THE ULTIMATE GUIDE TO BEING A GIRL

ON LOVE, BODY IMAGE, SCHOOL, AND MAKING IT THROUGH LIFE

CHRISTINA DE WITTE
WITH CHROSTIN

RP | TEENS
PHILADELPHIA

FOR EMMELIEN, MY MUSE

Running Press Teens
Hachette Book Group
1290 Avenue of the Americas, New York, NY 10104
www.runningpress.com/rpkids
@RP_Kids

Printed in the United States of America

First Edition: August 2018

Published by Running Press Teens, an imprint of Perseus Books, LLC, a subsidiary of Hachette Book Group, Inc. The Running Press Teens name and logo is a trademark of the Hachette Book Group.

The Hachette Speakers Bureau provides a wide range of authors for speaking events. To find out more, go to www.hachettespeakersbureau.com or call (866) 376-6591.

The publisher is not responsible for websites (or their content) that are not owned by the publisher.

Print book cover and interior design by
Frances J. Soo Ping Chow.

Library of Congress Control Number: 2017959792

ISBNs: 978-0-7624-9043-1 (paperback), 978-0-7624-9042-4 (ebook)

LSC-C

10 9 8 7 6 5 4 3 2 1

CONTENTS

PROLOGUE

Disclaimer: this is not the *ultimate* survival guide to being a girl.

N ow, before you head back to the store and slam this book on the counter, yelling something like, "I didn't order this! Give me my money back!" first hear me out.

I'm not here to tell you how to live your life—as a girl, as a teenager, or as a human being. I'm here to talk about *my* experiences as a teenage girl and to share some of the stuff that I went through when I was around your age.

Now, I literally just got out of puberty myself . . . or did I? Is it ever *really* over? Who knows? But here's the point I'm trying to make: my memories from "back in the day" are still fresh. As I'm writing this, I'm twenty years old. To some of you, twenty might seem ancient; to others, I'm practically an embryo. I'm good with both.

A couple years ago, I started drawing Chrostin as a getaway from the real world. Chrostin is essentially a funnier, more extroverted version of the real me. Recently, I collected my teen-girl experiences and bundled them into this book. And *The Ultimate Survival Guide to Being a Girl* is an answer to all the puberty guides I used to read as a teenager. The trouble with those "helpful" books I was given by well-meaning adults was that they only talked about the physical changes you go through as an adolescent, like growing pubic hair and battling acne.

I discovered firsthand that there's a lot more to puberty than just the physical stuff. Being a teenage girl can be harsh. You will be judged all the time—at school, at work, out in public. You'll think that you have a best friend, but then she'll stab you in the back. Perhaps you'll be bullied, just like many other teens. You'll be sad, happy, and angry all at the same time. Why? You don't know, and that makes you even more confused.

I wanted to create a book that *also* talks about the other stuff teens deal with—like mental health and diversity—because those are the things you don't learn about at school. Look, I don't have it all figured out. I'm still growing up myself. In all likelihood, I'll have to consult this book, too, from time to time, especially when I'm having a meltdown. I'll read it just to remind myself that it's okay to have bad days—that it's normal to get confused by the things that happen around you every day.

So, how does this book work?

You can read it on the toilet, on the train, in the waiting room at the doctor's office, during your lunch break, at your grandma's house, in your bed before you go to sleep—you get the point. This book can be read anytime, anyplace. I've divided it into ten chapters. We'll start really close to ourselves, by exploring our minds and bodies, before working our way outward to look at how we deal with others and with society in general. You choose where you start: whether you want to read it front to back or back to front, or check out all the comics and drawings first. There's no chronological order, so you can put it down and pick it back up whenever you feel like it.

Are you ready for a journey into womanhood?

Chapter One

MENTAL STUFF

Everything we do, think, or feel starts in our heads. That's why this book begins by exploring the very center of who we are: our brain and all the mental stuff we deal with as teenagers.

WHERE YOU DRAW THE LINE ON BEING HONEST

I'm sorry to break it to you, but we all lie. And hey, as long as you're not hiding a dead body in your backyard, there's not necessarily anything wrong with that. We also change our minds a lot. That doesn't make us liars; rather, it makes us human beings. But when it comes to honesty, do we really *need* to tell everybody everything? Do other people really need to know the unembellished truth always?

Flash back to when I was thirteen: I went shopping for clothes with the person I believed to be my best friend at the time. After browsing the racks for a while, we made our way to the fitting rooms to try on our items. We were, like I said, thirteen. But my friend was more "grown-up" than I was, and by that I mean she already had a D-cup bra at age eleven. It didn't make her life easy; I can tell you that.

To make a long story short, she was trying on an incredibly hideous (and I mean, truly *cringeworthy*) top and then *insert dramatic music* she asked for my opinion: did it look good on her?

It didn't.

I freaked out, because I'd never told her a single lie in the many years we'd been friends. And now I had the following options in which to answer my best friend:

1. Be honest and tell her the top didn't look good on her. This may have hurt her feelings, but at least she'd make the right decision and ditch the ugly top. Best friends don't let each other run around in unflattering attire, right? Right?!
2. Tell her I didn't necessarily *dislike* it, but that I prefer a different top she'd tried on before. With this response, I avoided having to make a negative comment about this shirt by saying something positive and nice about a different shirt. See what I did there? I didn't have to be a mean bitch to my friend and I still saved her the embarrassment of being seen in public wearing that atrocity of a top. Win-win!
3. Wait and gauge her reaction—see how she felt about the top herself. Before she got the chance to ask me, I'd jump in and ask *her*: "Well, what do you think?" If I was lucky, she'd tell me she hated it as much as I do. If not, I'd improvise.
4. Immediately tell her she looked beautiful in everything she tried on. I wanted my friend to feel good about herself, and if I had to tell a lie for that, it was for a good cause.

There's no right or wrong answer here. The truth is that we are often nicer to other people than we are to ourselves. At least, we like to think we are. Sometimes it's okay to hold your tongue or even tell a little white lie to avoid hurting people's feelings.

DISHONEST COMPLIMENT:

HONEST OPINION:

We lie about tons of things and for a variety of reasons, such as:

- sparing people's feelings (like when your friend shows up with an awful new haircut . . .);
- discussing our past (sure, I did volunteer work when I was twelve and spent my days rescuing baby kittens . . .);
- keeping our friend's secrets (nobody's 100-percent safe, except my bestie); or
- avoiding looking ungrateful (when a friend made you a drawing and it's hella ugly, but you have to appreciate the effort, although you never want to see it again. Not. Ever.).

There are times we choose to lie to protect others, and there are times we don't. Sometimes we choose to be frank and just tell it like it is. People might mistake you for a bitch, but remember: there's a difference between being mean and being truthful. Also, calling someone a bitch for giving their honest opinion doesn't qualify as being nice, either, even if that person swears she'd never lie to a friend.

If you ask me, being honest is great. People will value you and your opinion more because they know you'll tell the truth. But remember: it's okay to tell a little fib sometimes. Suppose your sister just had a baby and you don't think the child is adorable or cute *at all*. What do you do? Most likely, you won't go telling your sister that her offspring is positively hideous—for fear of hurting her and causing irreparable damage to your relationship. So, not telling the (whole) truth is perfectly okay at times, as long as you don't go overboard with it. Just remember: you'll quickly lose credibility if you lie constantly, so always do so sparingly and about things that aren't über-important.

COPING WITH FAILURE

"If I don't have a car, a great job, a family, and a beautiful home by the age of twenty-five, I'm a failure." "Unless I earn a lot of money, I don't feel like I'm successful in life." "If somebody doesn't like me, it means I messed up."

Do the above when-I-have-this-then-I'll-be-happy ways of thinking sound familiar to you? What if I told you that our lives could be *so* much easier if we let go of the impossible standards we set for ourselves?

We all want to be happy. I've never heard anyone complain about being *too* blessed or *too* content, have you? However (and this is the tricky part), no matter how happy we feel about ourselves, there's always *that one person* (you know the one) who seems even happier, and prettier, and cooler. . . . So we tend not to settle for what we have but keep aiming for something better, bigger. That's why we are

terribly hard on ourselves; nothing feels like it's good enough when we compare ourselves with others. We then feel this urge to fulfill the never-ending desire to be the best.

The key to avoiding this pitfall is *compassion*. And more specifically: self-compassion. When you are compassionate, you choose love over jealousy and anger. You choose love over the envy you feel when someone else has something you don't.

Compassion can also help you get over negative past experiences and rise above them. It's natural to be upset (and *remain* upset) about unpleasant things that happened to you. It's normal to hold a grudge against the people who caused you pain. But there's an alternative: instead of wallowing; you can try to accept that what's done is done. You can't turn back time, but you can choose to invest all this negative energy you have in a more positive way. If you learn to simply let things slide sometimes, you'll feel freer and more relaxed. Just let it go.

Did you know that holding on to anger can cause medical problems in the long run, too? Stress, burnout, hyperventilation, back problems, kidney problems, and many, many other nasty things can spring up due to pent-up anger. The bottom line: it's better for your mental and physical health to choose love, to forgive, and to leave some things in the past.

Loving yourself will also make it easier to cope with any failures and setbacks you might experience. When you think about it, every kind of experience will teach you something and enrich you in some meaningful way. Once you discover the silver lining of failure (you messed up, but you learned something!), it isn't that bad anymore. Once you realize that failing is a part of life, it won't feel like the end of the world but rather an avenue toward learning new things. After all, if we never make mistakes, how on earth are we supposed to learn from them?

Failure, pain, rejection . . . everyone makes mistakes and everyone gets hurt sometimes. Although we tend to believe that the super successful people we admire never fail and never have to deal with rejection, that assumption couldn't be further from the truth. J. K. Rowling is my all-time favorite example. Did you know that her manuscript was rejected *twelve* times by book publishers? What if she'd called it quits after the eleventh rejection? Well, thankfully she didn't. And her Harry Potter series went on to sell more than 100 million copies. You go, girl!

Whatever adolescent life throws at you, try to accept that a failure or setback doesn't define who you are. *You* are not a failure; you just made a mistake. Don't question yourself because of it—that can seriously shake your self-esteem and confidence. Also, you need to remember that you can't change the past, but you *can* shape your future. The sooner you take a step toward positivity, the sooner you'll be able to let go of all the bad stuff.

THE WIDE SPECTRUM OF EXTROVERSION AND INTROVERSION

Introverts and extroverts. Carl Jung, a Swiss psychiatrist and psychoanalyst, coined those concepts in the early twentieth century. Unfortunately, we have been using the terms to categorize people ever since, and that's a mistake. Here's why: it is a misconception to believe that a person is *either* an introvert or an extrovert. Being introverted or extroverted is more of a continuous spectrum. You are not strictly one or the other, and your position on the scale may vary from day to day.

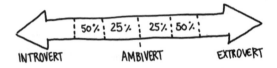

"There is no such thing as a pure extrovert or a pure introvert. Such a man would be in the lunatic asylum."

—Carl Jung

Most people don't strongly self-identify as introverted or extroverted, and thus are considered ambiverts. People who are ambiverts have both introverted and extroverted tendencies. I am an ambivert myself. For example, I'm very outgoing, but I also tend to get really nervous when I have to meet someone I don't know. I love chatting and talking over the phone, but my hands get clammy when I receive an incoming call from an unknown number. I love meeting new friends, but I hate taking the first step. I can be very social, but I enjoy being antisocial, too, as I appreciate my alone time.

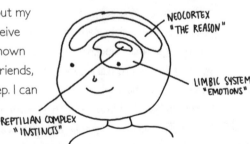

The difference between introverts and extroverts is a chemical. As you may know, our brain has the capacity to create a feel-good hormone called dopamine. We all have different levels of dopamine-fueled stimulation in our neocortex.

People who have naturally high levels of stimulation tend to be introverts—they are cautious about getting overstimulated to avoid anxiety or stress. People who have a lower level of stimulation, on the other hand, can get bored easily and will look for external impulses to raise their level of dopamine stimulation, or in human

EXTROVERTS

CAN BE A GOOD LISTENER, TOO

NOT NECESSARILY HAPPIER THAN INTROVERTS

LIKES TO BE ALONE SOME-TIMES, TOO

CARES ABOUT WHAT YOU THINK

CAN BE NERVOUS ABOUT SPEAKING IN PUBLIC, TOO

DOESN'T WANT TO BE THE CENTER OF ATTENTION

IS SHY SOMETIMES

INTROVERTS

NOT ALWAYS SHY

KNOWS HOW TO MAKE FUN, TOO

LIKES TO TALK, TOO

NOT NECESSARILY GEEKY

DOESN'T HATE PEOPLE!

DOESN'T WANT TO BE ALONE CONSTANTLY

NOT LESS OF A LEADER

HAS EMOTIONS AS WELL

speak: to feel good. Ambiverts will experience a bit of both, depending on the situation. Sometimes you'll long for action and excitement; other times you'll want to block out stimuli to protect yourself and give yourself a rest. Both are fine, as long as you listen to your body and your mind!

THE ART OF (NOT) GIVING UP ON THINGS

It's a hard-knock life for teenagers. Do you sometimes feel like you've been trying so hard to achieve something, but it's just not working out? Like you've poured your heart and soul into something you really want, but the many hours of hard work and effort just don't seem to pay off? You may have made a little progress, but the result is nowhere near what you'd hoped or imagined.

I personally believe everyone has at least one point in her life where she feels like giving up—like throwing in the towel and calling it quits. I think we can often see the appeal of it depending on the situation. Keep in mind that this feeling is pretty much universal, so whoever you turn to for support in your hour of need will have no problem relating to your situation. Sometimes, a good cry on a sympathetic shoulder is all you need to get your motivation back. Unfortunately, there's other times when—sigh—that's just not enough to get you back on track.

I remember going through a very difficult time when I was in my senior year of college. I had to juggle schoolwork and Chrostin work, writing this book, and planning my first big Chrostin event. I had my final school project to finish and a business to run, and it wasn't a walk in the park. Everything went so fast, and I worked long hours. One day, I got out of bed and immediately felt incredibly weak and dizzy. Like, as soon as I got up, I had to lie down again. My back and hands hurt so much, I couldn't draw for a while. It scared the shit out of me. What if this was *dum dum dum* a burnout?

I wanted to get on top of the situation quickly, so I went to see a doctor as soon as I could. He told me I "worked too much without allowing myself a break now and then." In order to get all my stuff done, I'd been denying myself some much needed me-time.

"Do you breathe properly?" he asked.

"Breathe?" I said.

"People often forget how important breathing is. Do you feel like you can't catch your breath sometimes? Like you're out of breath for no reason?"

"Sometimes. When I feel a panic attack coming on."

"Aha. Did you know that you can prevent panic attacks by learning how to breathe correctly?"

Clearly, I didn't know that. But I took his advice, and I've been feeling a lot better since that day.

It soon hit me that I had been working toward one big goal and had lost sight of the smaller milestones along the way. My ultimate goal was so far removed from what I was achieving day by day that I constantly felt like giving up. It just seemed so unrealistic, like I was never going to make it in the end. Luckily, my body warned me in time; I had to take a break.

It is important to take time for yourself sometimes—not just to rest, but also to celebrate your small successes. Don't put off rewarding yourself until you've reached the end of the road, or you'll struggle to stay motivated for the days, weeks, and maybe even months it may take you to get there. Treat yourself! Treating yourself can mean something different to each person. What do you consider a great reward? Is it a shopping trip? A dessert? A certain necklace you've been wanting for so long? Remember that treating yourself is purely for you, and you should not worry about money, calories, or others things in that moment. You deserve something nice every now and then.

When you're busy, you tend to forget to celebrate the little victories and accomplishments because you're too preoccupied with ticking off items on your to-do list. I used to be oh-so-proud to tell others that I was super busy. Busy, busy, busy. Too busy to attend that barbecue or a night out with friends. I was working toward something. I had a goal. I was focused. But was I happy? Not at all.

Nowadays, I make sure to schedule some me-time every week: a digital detox, a long hot bath, a walk, a Netflix night, a trip into the city or to the mall. I find that it's a lot easier to maintain my motivation in the long run if I allow myself some time to relax and look back on all the minor milestones I've achieved. It's so much easier to chase your dreams if you charge your batteries every now and again. You don't see a car driving from point A to B without fuel, do you?

When you're having a tough time and you're tempted to give up, try to remember why you started in the first place. Make a list if you have to. Revive the motivation and enthusiasm you had in the beginning so you'll be able to make it to the finish line.

Oh, and do you breathe properly? Read more about helpful breathing exercises in the section about social anxieties on pages 25-26.

ME, TREATING MYSELF AFTER 15 MINUTES OF STUDYING

BREAKING THROUGH THAT COMFORT ZONE

Friday May 19, 2017. My friend called to ask if we could hang out and grab some dinner for her birthday. Birthday dinner? Yes, please!

"Of course! I would love to. Who's coming?" I asked.

"Oh, just a few people. Nothing fancy," she said.

"Do I know them?"

"Um, you know me. And everyone's going to adore you."

"Heh, okay. See you tonight."

Oh no. I had this conversation at 2:00 p.m., and the dinner wouldn't start until 7:00 p.m., giving me a solid five hours to panic. I completely freaked out because the idea of meeting new people gives me crippling anxiety. I had to find an excuse not to go. The people my friend hangs out with are *cool* people. Like, overly social and famous and relaxed and . . . hold on! What was I doing? I was overthinking this again. I needed to get a grip. I needed to pull myself together before I left my house. This was me, dreading the prospect of having to leave my comfort zone.

A comfort zone is a situation, position, or level that someone feels comfortable and confident in. Everything you do that doesn't excite you or doesn't give you anxiety is part of your comfort zone. Perhaps you've heard that stepping out of your comfort zone can be good for you. But here's a *whole list* of reasons why leaving your cocoon is beneficial for you:

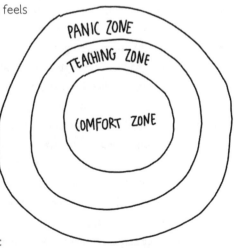

1. Your comfort zone will gradually expand if you exceed your boundaries sometimes. Every little step you take out of your zone will help you feel more comfortable with unfamiliar stuff in life. It teaches you to adapt and get used to new situations.

2. You learn new things. Your brain will stimulate your dopamine levels (the stuff that makes us happy and satisfied, remember?) and encourage you to continue doing whatever it is you're doing. We tend to look for the middle ground, where we feel a little bit anxious but not too much. When you feel less stressed and more comfortable, you've successfully expanded your comfort zone. Congrats!

3. You'll grow more curious about other stuff in life and the world in general. Doing something you've never done before will fuel your curiosity.

So, meeting new people is not necessarily a bad thing. How much you can (or want to) extend your comfort zone at a given time is absolutely up to you, and only you. That said, there will inevitably come a time when you have to be brave and face a scary, new situation. That's why I'll provide some tips and tricks that helped me broaden my horizons and expand my comfort zone:

- Say, "Screw it! What have I got to lose?" and do the thing.
- Find someone to help/motivate/accompany you. Sharing an experi-ence can lower the threshold and make a scary situation less, well, scary. For example, take a friend to a networking event. You'll notice it's not that bad. Go on your own the next time and think of it as a new level in expanding your comfort zone.
- Prepare yourself mentally. Preparation is key. What can you expect from the situation you're about to put yourself in? What's the worst-case scenario? The more scenarios you anticipate, the fewer surprises you'll run into.
- Challenge yourself each day to do or learn something new. Smile at

people when you are outside walking; don't just stare at the ground. Order something you've never ordered before at a restaurant. Take a different route to school. Clean your room and throw everything out that you haven't used in a year. Go out and start a conversation. Listen to different kinds of music. Try a new hairstyle.

Don't know where to start? Try out this cool online tool called whatismycomfortzone.com. After a short survey about your professional life, lifestyle, and adrenaline consumption, the tool gives you some great and easy tips on how to extend your comfort zone.

STICK UP FOR YOURSELF!

At this point in my life, I think sticking up for myself comes down to being able to say no to people without seeming rude or impolite. In my experience, saying no and being rude are often treated as if they are the same thing. *They are not.* Especially when I was a teenager, I found it difficult to say what was on my mind. Today, I can say I'm more assertive. Yes, it took me many years of learning. No, it wasn't easy. But I no longer feel like people can walk all over me, so it was worth the effort I made as a teen to become more confident and self-assured.

HOW I FEEL AFTER THE 100TH TIME SAYING "YES" TO STUFF I DON'T LIKE

HOW I FEEL AFTER ONE TIME SAYING "NO"

Sticking up for yourself becomes even more difficult when the situation you're in involves people you are close to, like your best friend, your partner, or your teacher/boss. But you need to know why speaking up is important for your future (personal) life and career. The main reason is that it's easy for people to take advantage of you if you don't open your mouth and speak up. And we wouldn't want that, right?

Try to count how many times you've said yes this week to things you actually wanted to say no to. If you have zero times, congratulations! You can skip this section altogether and move on with your carefree life. If you've counted more than five, I think we should have a talk. Perhaps you don't want to hear what comes next, but I promise it'll make you feel better in the end.

It may seem like a good idea to make the following resolution: you'll never again promise to do something you don't want to—not ever. If you feel completely and totally uncomfortable with what you are asked to do, that is absolutely the right way to go. More power to ya! The reality is often more ambiguous and complex, however, and there'll be times when you'll feel inclined to agree to things you'd rather say no to. And that's okay. Sometimes people will ask for something without necessarily meaning to take advantage of you. Such requests are called *favors*, and here are a few examples of them:

• When your best friend calls and needs you, but you don't feel like socializing. You would appreciate it if she respected your need to be alone, but you talk to her anyway.

• When your sweetheart has a very boring family dinner coming up. Although you know it's going to be boring and his/her family will most likely ask you the most embarrassing questions, it's what you do for your partner in crime.

• When your best friend asks you to help him move. Everyone knows that moving involves a lot of stress, sweat, and lower-back pain. But it's your best friend, and he will reward you by returning the favor when you need it.

Now that you know when it's okay to say yes, here are some ways to say no when it's really necessary:

- No.
- No, thanks.
- No way.
- No way, José. (This one's extra funky.)
- Not for all the tea in China.
- Only when pigs fly.

All kidding aside, saying no is actually a matter of training yourself how to do it. When you say it for the first time, you'll feel both empowered and slightly guilty. Try to find a balance between being super selfish and being utterly selfless. The more unwanted tasks you manage to eliminate, the happier you'll be. Think of all the extra time you'll have for the things you actually enjoy doing . . . and for those mildly unpleasant things for the benefit of your loved ones.

ABOUT (ACCEPTING) FLAWS

Accepting your flaws is an important step toward achieving personal success and becoming comfortable with yourself. Flaws can make you feel very aware and self-conscious of yourself. Knowing and understanding that there's no such thing as a perfect human being is a great first step to accepting who you are, flaws and all.

I had to look up the definition of a flaw—which is a noun— and here's what I found: any small to large human imperfection in a behavior and/or a characteristic and/or an imperfection in a subset(s). Flaws are very personal and can be everything about yourself that makes you feel weird about who you are.

Flaws can ultimately become our strengths, because they make us the unique person we are. Without our flaws, we would be perfectly complete human beings and that would make us even weirder. Also, the things you consider flaws can be a reason for someone else to like you.

In 2011, when I was almost sixteen, I met a random guy at my high school. We were the same age but were not in the same class. So, I didn't really know him, but I always thought he was kinda cute. As we started seeing more of each other, we grew closer, and eventually he became my first boyfriend. I remember being so shy because I'd never kissed someone before. I considered my total lack of experience a shortcoming—it made me feel insecure. Luckily, he is a great guy and my "flaw" (not being an experienced kisser) was never an issue in our relationship. We were able to learn from each other, and that is the most important thing. In hindsight, I feel silly for beating myself up over my inexperience in the kissing department. It wasn't a real flaw after all (and practicing was a highly efficient solution).

Another set of self-professed flaws we have to deal with are those that have to do with our appearance. How do you tackle those? First of all, remember that what you consider a flaw is often something another person a) has never even noticed before, until you point it out, or b) may find cute or attractive about you. Of course, you don't have to *look good* for other people, but you do have to *feel good* for yourself.

I always used to have a bit more hair growth than the average girl. Especially on my legs, arms, and facial area. When I was younger, I did gymnastics and absolutely adored wearing the standard-issue leotards. I loved choosing a new print when I'd outgrown the previous one. That is, until one day, when this guy on my team pointed out that I had a bunch of arm hair. You know what? He was right, I did. But the way he said it made it sound as if it were a really bad thing. A dirty thing. Something to be ashamed of. Another girl from our group stood up for me, immediately replying that she "thought it was cute" and jokingly adding that "it was warmer for the winter." Although the girl who defended me didn't think my hairiness was a flaw, I decided it was from that day onward.

For as long as I remember, I've struggled with the way I look. I have a love-hate relationship with my Asian roots, because they made me look different than most people at my school. Did I feel different growing up? Yes, because people kept pointing out that I was different, for whatever reason (as if I wasn't acutely aware of it already). As a result, my being different made me feel like less of a person at times, like I was worth less than the others. Which is completely ridiculous, I know. Your looks don't (and won't ever) define your qualities as a friend, an employee, a student, or a person, and they most definitely don't determine your worth.

Here are some practical tips for turning your flaws into something great:

- Every night, write down things that you like about yourself. List three things that you've done well that day and three things you like about your appearance. You'll soon notice that there's no connection between your achievements and how you look. But it is important that you feel good about both aspects of your person.

- Tackle your bad habits. For example, do you smoke? Bad habits are often a coping mechanism because they give you a false sense of control. Take *real* control and get rid of the stuff that's bad for you!

~~FLAWS~~
UNIQUE FEATURES

~~TOO AVERAGE~~
UNIQUE

~~TOO HAIRY~~
UNIQUE

~~TOO FAT~~
UNIQUE

~~TOO SHORT~~
UNIQUE

~~TOO BIG~~
UNIQUE

- Find something you're really good at. Are you musical? Then learn to play an instrument. Do you love to draw? Then go to art school or take a summer drawing class. Find your thing and develop your skills. The same goes for your looks: enhance the features you like. I guarantee that's a way to help you embrace the ones you don't.

SOCIAL ANXITIES AND HOW TO DEAL WITH THEM

Earlier, I told you the story of how I learned to step out of my comfort zone. When my friend asked me to join a birthday party where I didn't know anyone except for her, my social anxiety kicked in almost immediately. My heart rate skyrocketed. My palms became sweaty. My thoughts went in overdrive. . . . What was wrong with me?

Social anxiety is the fear of being judged and evaluated negatively by other people, and it leads to feelings of inadequacy, inferiority, embarrassment, humiliation, and depression. And social phobia (another term for Social Anxiety Disorder) is the third-largest mental health-care problem in the *world*. That's right.

HOW SOCIAL PHOBIA MIGHT FEEL:

→ ALL OF THESE THOUGHTS IN 30 SECONDS ←

You could argue that everyone gets a bit nervous at times and in certain social contexts. But social phobia is more than just being shy. People with a true social phobia tend to experience distress in the following situations: meeting new people, making small talk, being the center of attention, going on a date, taking exams, speaking in front of a crowd, being watched or criticized, etc. They may feel extremely uncomfortable, insecure, and self-conscious when they have to walk, eat, or make a phone call in a public space. People with social anxiety can experience this so intensely that they may prefer to avoid social interaction to keep their stress level to a minimum.

The great news is that social phobia is fully treatable with effective therapy, patience, and dedication. You may want to try to control your anxiety on your own first, so here are some effective tips to help you tackle your phobia step-by-step:

1. Call yourself out on being a Negative Nancy. The problem with negative thoughts is that they're like self-fulfilling prophecies: if you start out by thinking you're going to screw up, you're setting yourself up for failure from the beginning. A negative mindset won't help you overcome anything. Try to look more realistically at social situations instead of feeding your fears. For example, if you have to do an oral presentation in front of your class, remind yourself that people probably won't even notice that you're nervous because they don't care as much about the presentation as you do.

2. Shake off the thought that everyone is watching you. Everyone is *not* watching you. Focus on being genuine and attentive, rather than being perfect. Try to be present in the moment and listen to what is happening around you. But try not to think about what others are thinking because you can't truly know what is inside another person's head.

3. Change your lifestyle. Did you know that a more active lifestyle reduces stress and anxiety? Me neither! Try to drink less coffee, tea, soda, or energy drinks, as they contain a lot of caffeine and sugar. You may find such stimulants stimulating, but they can also stimulate anxiety symptoms! Drink plenty of water, go for a run or a long walk, and get enough sleep. If I don't sleep for at least eight hours a night, I automatically feel more stressed the next day.

4. Learn to control your breath. Overbreathing (like when you're hyperventilating) can lead to physical symptoms of anxiety, such as dizziness, increased heart rate, and muscle tension. Meditation could be a great option for learning to control your breathing.

a. Slow breathing can help you relieve anxiety and prevent a panic attack. If breathing relaxation is something new to you, it may be easiest to practice lying flat on your back with knees bent and feet flat on the floor and slightly placed apart.
b. Next, place one hand on your chest and the other on your abdomen.
c. Hold your breath and count to ten. Then, breathe out firmly and think *relax* to yourself.
d. Inhale slowly through your nose for three seconds. You'll notice that your hand on your abdomen should rise while the hand on your chest is relatively still.
e. Then, exhale through your mouth for three seconds, making that *whooshing* sound as you breathe out. Again, think *relax* to yourself. Now, the hand on your abdomen should fall as you exhale.
f. After a full minute of breathing this way, hold your breath again for ten full seconds. Repeat this process for five minutes. Once you feel like you have the hang of it lying down, you can start practicing slow breathing sitting or even standing. You can even control your breath in public.

Sometimes, though, self-help isn't enough. Make sure to check with your doctor if you feel you might benefit from professional medical guidance, like therapy or medication. If you want to learn more about social phobia, make sure to check out HelpGuide.org. You can find tons of practical tips on how to stop worrying, to release stress, to become more social, and more. Just remember: social phobia is nothing to be ashamed of. A lot of people suffer from it, but you can get the symptoms under control. If you apply the previous tips and remember how to control your breath, you will take a big step forward. Go you!

GRABS BACK

Chapter Two

THE BEAUTY OF THE HUMAN BOOTY

As a teenager, I struggled a lot with how I looked—with the clothes I wanted to wear and with how I wished I looked like someone else. This chapter deals with some important questions you might have about our awesome pubescent female bodies—and will hopefully inspire you to see the beautiful person in each one of us.

DETERMINING YOUR BODY TYPE

Think about this: no two bodies on this planet are identical. Each and every one of our bodies is absolutely unique. People all over the world come in millions of different sizes and shapes. Isn't that the most beautiful thing? But, then, why do I still feel so weird about my own shape? Why can't I just accept the way I look and go on with my life? Appreciating the great diversity of body shapes is the first step toward accepting your own.

First of all, it's important to understand that what you see in the media nowadays isn't representative of what bodies *really* look like. Take Taylor Hill, a supermodel who is absolutely flawless wherever she appears. For her shoots, however, she's surrounded by a large team of personal trainers, stylists, makeup artists, and other professionals. Her pictures are retouched in Photoshop to cover up blemishes and imperfections. What we see on billboards and magazine covers is not real life. Real life is the same Taylor sitting on the couch at home without makeup, maybe even watching *Stranger Things* just like the rest of us.

THE MOST COMMON BODY TYPES
(ACCORDING TO FASHION WEBSITES)

HOURGLASS:
- EMPHASIZE THE WAIST
- TRY: CROP TOPS, PENCIL SKIRTS, WRAP DRESSES, WIDE-LEGGED PANTS ...

APPLE:
- FOCUS ON THE SHOULDERS / LEGS
- TRY: LONG COATS, HIGH WAIST SWING SKIRTS, LOW WAIST CIGAR PANTS ...

RECTANGLE:
- HIGHLIGHT THE SMALLEST PART OF YOUR WAIST, SO YOUR HIPS AND SHOULDERS ARE MORE PROPORTIONAL
- TRY: RUFFLED TOPS, CROPPED JACKETS, TAPERED PANTS...

PEAR:
- BALANCE YOUR FIGURE
- TRY: OFF-THE-SHOULDER TOPS, A-LINE SKIRTS, BOOT CUT PANTS, FLARE DRESSES...

THERE ARE MANY VARIATIONS TO THESE BASIC SHAPES:

INVERTED TRIANGLE

FULL HOURGLASS

LEAN COLUMN

PIZZA

When it comes to understanding and accepting your body, you may want to take a look at different body types first. It's not always your size or shape that matters: the fit of your clothes plays an equally important role in how you look and feel about yourself. Rather than shopping for trends, you can look for clothes that flatter your body type; they'll make you feel comfortable and confident. There are plenty of beautiful clothing lines for all body types nowadays (hooray!), so you'll definitely find some awesome pieces that fit you like a glove.

I used to be completely focused on the parts of my body that I *didn't* like, but it's important to see your body as a *whole*. Dare to look in the mirror and describe what you see. Try to be as objective as you possibly can. Perhaps you have fairly long legs? Or relatively short ones? Maybe you never noticed that you have awesome collar bones or a long, elegant neck or a beautiful waistline?

Don't be afraid to examine your body. That's how you discover the parts you like the most, so you can enhance them. It took me a few years to get there, but I absolutely love how I look now. I learned to embrace my Asian roots more. I've accepted that I'm not perfect, but that's okay because nobody is.

Not sure what your body type is? I've listed a few examples. Of course, it's perfectly possible that you don't fully identify with one of these but find yourself somewhere in the middle between two (or even three or more) types. That's cool, too!

MY THIGHS LOOK LIKE THE SIZE OF TEXAS WHEN SEATED

Obviously, Texas is huge and my thighs are not *that* big. But my hips don't lie. I used to be a real stick figure when I was thirteen. Over the course of the next two years, though, boobs started to pop out. Hips started to expand. My waistline morphed into a bizarre shape. What was happening? I did not order this. Can I speak to the manager, please?

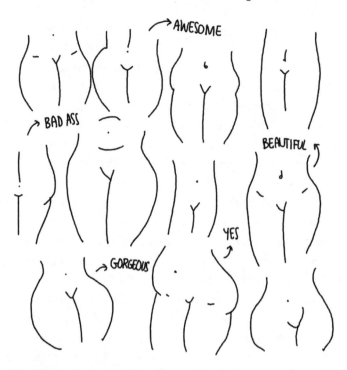

It's called puberty, and literally everybody has to go through this.
But back to your beautiful body. Whatever they look like, there are *always* reasons to love your thighs. Thighs are truly wonderful. They helped our mothers with giving birth to us. Laps are awesome because puppies can fall asleep on them. Whether they are naturally small, medium, or large, your hips and thighs are beautiful things for you to embrace and enjoy.

WEARING CLOTHING, EVEN IF IT DOESN'T FIT THAT WELL

When I was in high school, I used to wear oversized shirts to cover my female curves. I didn't wear makeup until I was sixteen. I even wanted to be a boy sometimes. I used to be jealous of the fact that boys simply have to unzip their pants in order to pee. There was something laid-back and casual about boys, and this lead me to believe that there wasn't as much pressure on them when it came to their looks, friendships, grades, etc. I thought life would be a lot easier as a boy.

My tomboy phase came and went quickly. It was more of a tough facade I'd constructed to protect myself. I didn't want to *be* an actual boy; I wanted to become the girl I'd always wanted to be but never had had the chance to before. Slowly, I gave up skateboarding, started wearing different clothes, and did my first experiments with makeup. I felt like I was blooming.

But, apparently, not everyone in my so-called girl gang was equally thrilled about the transformation I was undergoing. A few girls bullied me. It started with exclusion. Turning their backs when I approached. Sending hateful texts. Ignoring what I was saying. Gossiping about me so I could hear. Giving me nasty looks in the hallway. All the crappy shit.

The reason for the bullying? They couldn't keep up with the changes I was experiencing and embracing. I was finally happy, but they weren't digging that. It was confusing to me. Was I supposed to go back to the old version of myself, someone I didn't want to be anymore, just to make my friends happy?

The answer was no. Hell no. Things escalated when I wore a skirt for the first time. Gosh, you should have seen some of the girls' faces. They were angry with me because "I didn't stay true to myself." Girl, let me tell you this: don't let *anyone* tell you who you are or how you should feel about the clothes *you* want to wear. You are in charge of your own body and your own person. Be the person you want to be and feel you are, no matter what anyone else says or thinks.

As I slowly grew apart from the negative people in my life, I started to feel freer. I played around with different styles and makeup looks. Nothing feels greater than discovering your own style. I have to admit my experiments weren't always very flattering or cute, but trying new things was the only way to find my own personal look, which I now feel confident and wear with pride.

CHOOSING A TATTOO: THE DOS AND DON'TS

Tattoos can be enhancing, and they often carry a very special meaning. Other than being aesthetic or symbolic, they're also pretty . . . permanent. Before I tell you about the steps you should take in preparation for getting inked, I'd like to inform you some more about what tattooing actually is.

A tattoo is a form of body modification, because it changes the way your body looks. A design (usually a very personal one) is transferred onto the dermis layer of the skin using a rapidly moving needle with ink to change the pigment of your skin. Before someone can call themselves an official tattoo artist, they must have years of practice and a number of certificates and qualifications. A tattoo shop has to be perfectly in line with strict hygienic guidelines as well in order to operate.

Even if you've been thinking about getting a tattoo for a very long time, from a legal perspective, you have to be at least eighteen years old in the United States to be green-lighted for a tattoo without parental consent. The regulation for minors differs from state to state. You may need a written consent from your parent or guardian, or you may need them to be present with you during the procedure. The reason for this is that, according to the law, minors aren't equipped to make a decision that is this drastic and life-changing. A tattoo may *seem* cool, but you really have to think twice about making a choice this big. If you woke up one morning thinking it might be awesome to get a tattoo, you probably want to hit the breaks and take some time to think about it first. No matter how much fun it is, planning a tattoo requires a lot more than choosing a fun design that you like at the moment. It's something that will stay with you for the rest of your life.

Of course, I'm not here to tell you what you can and can't do (you do you, girl), but regretting a tattoo is the last thing you want. If you live with your parents, you need to make sure to at least inform them of your plans. If they are not the tattoo-loving type, you should do them the courtesy of involving them in the process. If nothing else, it will help them get used to the idea. I made the mistake of simply coming home one day with permanent ink on my arm. My brilliant reasoning was that my dad wouldn't be able to do anything about it once it was done. (He could hardly rub the ink off my arm, now could he?) . . . But needless to say, I got the biggest earful of my life.

If you *have* thought it through and *have* discussed this with your guardians if you're under eighteen, and you *still* can't sleep at night because you're so overly excited about a tattoo, you are probably ready to start your decision-making process. I collected the following tips with the help of my tattoo artist, and I trust they won't have you ending up with a pizza tat on your forehead. Please don't disappoint me.

1. MAKE SURE YOU MEET THE CRITERIA.
You need to remember that you're not allowed to get a tattoo if:
• you're a minor (reread the section above to find out why)

- you're a minor and you *have* consent but are found to be too young by the tattoo artist (they have the right to turn you down if they feel you're not ready for the procedure)
- you're drunk or high on drugs
- you're allergic to the ink (talk about this with your doctor and artist if you have any known allergies)

2. BE EXTRA CAREFUL ABOUT THE TATTOO DESIGN YOU CHOOSE.

- If you choose a tattoo that includes text, make sure that the spelling is right. It's not the artist's fault if *you* left a spelling error or typo in the design.
- Be careful with foreign languages, especially ones that use different writing systems. Always make sure to double-check with a native speaker that you have spelled something correctly or have the phrase right. You'll regret taking Google Translate's word for it if your tattoo ends up spelling "sweet potato" in Chinese.
- Names. Unless they refer to a family member or someone who passed away, it's not a good idea. Friends, public figures/celebrities, and relationships change. Your tattoo doesn't.
- Anything that's a trend right now. Trends come and go very quickly.
- Anything that's offensive—I'm talking about offensive or racist symbols, images, or sayings.
- Everything Internet or memes. Just don't.

3. TTT: THINK. THIS. THROUGH.

Take your time. There's no need to rush. If you still want a tattoo after weeks of thinking and rethinking it, you know it's not a whim.

4. RESEARCH!

For many people, tattoos are works of art. And since they're so personal, you may want to do some research/soul-searching before you choose your design. Here are some things to think about as you explore what sort of tattoo design you want:
- Who or what inspires you?

- What style do you like? Check Pinterest for inspiration.
- Find a tattoo artist that suits you and your style. Take a good look at the artist's portfolio and set up a meeting to see them in person. You should feel comfortable and sure about the artist working on you. If you don't, keep looking for the right person. Don't feel pressured to settle for the first artist you encounter if they're not the right fit for you.
- There's only one rule of thumb here: don't get a tattoo on the cheap. A good tattoo is worth every penny, and the finished result will reflect the amount you paid for it. Adjust your budget, not your tattoo or your choice of artist.
- Consider where you want the tat placed on your body. Do you want it to be visible? Do you want to be able to cover it up for certain occasions? Think about how noticable you want it to be before you commit to inking yourself.

5. CREATE A DESIGN.

Artists appreciate it when you try to translate your ideas into a sketch or drawing. Don't worry about it being "ugly" or "unprofessional." I promise you: bringing a sketch or drawing makes it easier for the tattoo artist to understand what kind of design you have in mind. No one can read your thoughts, so make sure what you want is clearly communicated to the artist *before* the first needle prick.

6. BE PATIENT.

It may take some time before your favorite artist has an opening to schedule an appointment with you. Don't be surprised or disappointed if it takes weeks or even months before you can get your tattoo. As soon as all systems are a go and you've discussed your wishes, the artist will make a custom design for you. Don't be afraid to add adjustments or reject the proposal altogether—you're the one who has to wear it for the rest of your life. Take a few days to see how you feel about the design. Are you still sure? If so, then you're good to go!

7. GET INFORMED.

If you've come this far and are still as excited as you were in the beginning, you know you really want this and aren't just acting on an impulse.

Tattoo artists, even the most talented ones, are nothing without their tools. Let's take a look at what they use to create their permanent body art:

When the big day has finally arrived and you're ready to get inked, here's a couple of things that are good to know about the procedure and aftercare:

(SOME)
ESSENTIAL TOOLS YOUR TATTOO ARTIST USES

TATTOO MACHINE

STERILIZATION

INK

NEEDLES

POWER

MEDICAL SUPPLIES

GLOVES

AFTERCARE

• Getting a tattoo can hurt like a bitch or it can be almost pain-free. It all depends on the body part on which you choose to put your tat. As a general rule, tattoos that are placed on an area of skin that's close to the bone, such as your ribs, neck, spine, or collar bone, are the most painful, because there is less padding from muscles and fat. Also sensitive are the areas where your skin is really thin, such as the insides of your arms, your feet, and your hands. Remember that any tattoo will hurt a little bit. The good news is: the pain is temporary, the tattoo is forever. Yay!

- When your tattoo is done, the artist will cover it in plastic foil to protect your clothes for the remainder of the day. In the days and weeks after, some redness and swelling can occur on or around the tattooed skin, and that area might feel a little itchy. All of this is normal. Just stick to the aftercare routine recommended by your tattoo artist. This routine generally consists of applying a special cream to the tattoo a couple times a day.
- Avoid exposing your tattoo to the sun for the first few weeks/months. Too much sun can cause the design to blur or can make the colors fade. That would be a total waste, so make sure you always cover it up or at least wear sunscreen!
- If you're worried that something is wrong, don't hesitate to contact your artist for help or advice. They'll be happy to assist!

FIVE PRACTICAL TIPS TO HELP YOU FALL IN LOVE WITH YOUR BODY

One of the biggest questions I asked myself as a teenager is how the heck people get to the point where they feel confident about their bodies. While everybody else seemed absolutely beautiful and comfortable in her own skin, I just sat there feeling trapped in a package I didn't care for at all: my body.

If there's one thing I found myself struggling with over and over again, it was my body image. Unfortunately, I was one of the girls who was brainwashed by society's beauty standards. As a young girl with foreign roots, it was difficult to find people like me represented in mainstream media. Why didn't I look like the women on billboards, TV shows, or magazine covers? I couldn't identify with them, and that didn't exactly help my self-esteem.

I soon figured out that no one was going to change my body image for me; I would have to do the heavy lifting on my own. So I started to take care of myself as a part of my self-love process. I followed five tips that helped me improve my body image. I'll share them with you here:

HOW DID I LEARN TO ACCEPT MYSELF?

LISTENING TO MY BODY

FUELING MY BODY WITH YUMMY, HEALTHY FOODS

GETTING RID OF PEOPLE WHO MISTREATED ME ♡

UPDATING MY WARDROBE

STOPPED OBSESSING ABOUT MY WEIGHT

1. Get rid of people who constantly judge you for how you look. Seriously, you don't need that kind of negativity in your life. If you love you, other people will, too.

2. Listen to your body. Sometimes it tries to tell you things you don't want to ignore. Sleep enough. Get enough rest. Take time. Drink plenty of water. People tend to forget about their body's most basic needs.

3. Update your wardrobe. I got rid of the clothes that made me look like a potato and started looking for pieces that were cute and comfortable. I was unapologetic about the way I looked, and that felt so great!

4. Overcome your obsession with your weight (if you struggle with this, like I did). I figured I'd lost enough time freaking out about my "ideal body" and started living life instead. I found a new hobby. Walked around naked. Treated myself. Allowed myself to fall in love again.

5. Fuel your body with healthy yummy foods. I discovered the soothing and therapeutic effects of cooking, so I started to prepare more (and more balanced) meals for myself. Of course, I still allow myself to enjoy the occasional unhealthy snack in order to keep myself sane.

WHAT TO DO WHEN
YOUR EARRINGS SMELL NASTY

If you wear earrings, you've experienced this at least once in your life. You remove the earrings you've been wearing for the last couple of days. You're not sure why, but something tells you to take a good sniff. Nothing in your life could've prepared you for it, but there it is: the damn things smell like French cheese on a hot summer day.

If it seems as if even the most hygienic person can't avoid ear gunk, that's because it's perfectly natural. We all have it. As a matter of fact, it doesn't have much to do with your personal hygiene at all. It's natural for your body to secrete something called sebum, an oil-like substance that lubricates your skin and makes it waterproof. Sometimes, you can wipe the sebum off your jewelry and it looks like a thick, yellowish drop of goo. Yuck!

The good news is that you can minimize the unpleasant smell by following some very easy steps, which work for any kind of metal piercing:

- If your earring holes are completely healed, you can take your earrings off while you shower. Clean your piercing area with soap.
- Clean your body jewelry often. Metallic jewelry can easily be cleaned with warm water.
- You can pour a drop of natural lavender oil on your earrings to condition them.

Ta-dah! If you stick to this easy routine, the cheesy smell will be less noticeable.

WHY FEMININE HYGIENE PRODUCTS SHOULD BE FREE

This is a question I've been asking myself for so many years. Mother Nature gave us this beautiful thing called our period. This is what happens when a female body discharges stuff (blood and excess tissue) it no longer needs. It comes from the uterus, which prepares itself every month (depending on your cycle) to receive a fertilized egg by creating extra lining. If an egg is fertilized, it'll nestle in the uterus and the woman will be pregnant. If not, she'll have her menstruation or period. Is it natural? Yes. Is it weird? It can be a little bit weird the first time.

I had some questions about menstruating I didn't dare ask my friends or relatives.

Period Smells

Well, it shouldn't. Your period blood is the cleanest blood that will ever leave your body. Regardless, a strong, metallic odor can sometimes occur. Where does it come from? It happens when the period blood comes into contact with air. If you change your sanitary napkin or tampon frequently enough, there should be no unpleasant smells. Depending on the type of product you use, you should change it every couple of hours to make sure you are staying dry, hygenic, and un-smelly.

Using a Tampon Correctly

No period protection should hurt you. They are designed to make your period a bit more bearable while being as minimally invasive as possible. Look for the kind of product that best fits your needs. There's tons of available options on the market nowadays, so I'm sure you'll find your match!

Tampons come in different sizes and varieties to serve different purposes. There are daytime and nighttime tampons, tampons meant for exercising and sports, etc. Inserting a tampon might feel a little funny at first, but it shouldn't hurt. However, if a tampon feels uncomfortable to wear, there are a few alternatives you can try out.

In addition to tampons, you can try sanitary pads and menstruation cups. In general, there's two types of protection products: external protection products (sanitary pads) absorb the blood once it's outside of your body, whereas internal protection products (tampons and cups) are placed inside your vagina to collect menstrual blood and prevent it from leaving your body.

Both types are safe; you just have to figure out which type is most compatible with your lifestyle. Are you an active girl? Are you involved in a lot of sports? Consider trying a tampon or cup if you move a lot, because those can feel more secure. Whatever you do, always remember that the choice is completely up to you.

There is a slight risk of TSS (toxic shock syndrome), a disease that is related to tampon usage. But don't worry—the chances are absolutely minimal that you'll develop TSS, and if you change your tampon regularly (read the instructions to know exactly how often you should do this), you'll be perfectly fine!

But aren't tampons and sanitary pads bad for the environment, you might ask? If you're concerned about environmental issues, you can try alternative options to sanitary pads and tampons. Most of them are available in grocery stores or drugstores:

• **Nonchlorine bleached all-cotton pads and tampons:** They look like the conventional products, but they are organic and more

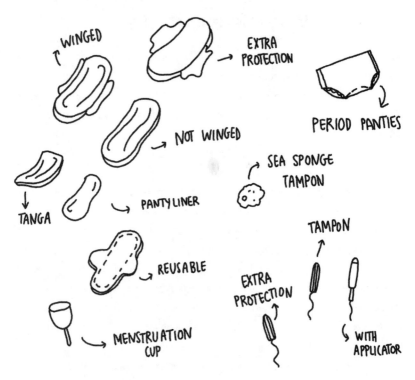

biodegradable, which also makes them a bit more expensive than their regular counterparts. Available in some of the larger supermarkets and online.

• *Reusable and washable pads and period panties:* Yes, they do exist! They work the same but instead of throwing them away, you wash them. They can be a little expensive at first, because you have to buy them in bulk, but you can reuse them for years. Also a great option for girls who are a little sensitive down below. Available in natural products stores and online.

• *Sea sponge tampons:* My mom uses these! They look like regular sponges but are actually harvested from the ocean. When you insert the sea sponge into your vagina, it absorbs the blood flow. The sponges aren't very expensive individually, but you have to change them frequently, just like regular tampons. Available in natural/bio stores and online.

The Whys of Paying for Feminine Hygiene Products

Feminine hygiene products are taxed as "luxury items." Yep, you read that right, and nope, I'm not kidding. The government thinks we bleed for fun, so they think it's reasonable to let us pay thousands of dollars to buy the accessories we need to stop the blood from squirting all over the place.

All kidding aside, millions of women worldwide don't even have access to period protection, and in India alone, 70 percent of reproductive health conditions are caused by poor menstrual hygiene. Luckily, more progressive countries are pioneering a number of programs to correct this injustice. In July 2017, Scotland started a six-month trial of free tampons and sanitary napkins, enabling low-income women in the city of Aberdeen access to free feminine hygiene products. Angela Constance, cabinet secretary, commented that it's simply unacceptable that some girls and women are forced to go without the sanitary products they need because they are struggling financially. The program is expected to help more than one thousand women in the city of Aberdeen. With this practical solution, Scotland is trying to help eradicate period poverty. Hopefully, many more countries worldwide will follow Scotland's lead in launching similar initiatives. Go, Scotland!

If you want to learn more about period protection, check out plannedparenthood.org and youngwomanshealth.org.

SHAVING 101

I remember being friends with a girl in ninth grade. Let's call her Alice, for the sake of the story. Alice was a blonde, and the hairs on her body were rather thin and light in color, so they were less visible and noticeable. Mine, on the contrary, were pitch-black and super thick. We were both fourteen, and a lot of girls in our class were experimenting with shaving and waxing. To me, the whole thing felt a bit weird, and I didn't really want to give it a try. Randomly attacking my legs with a razor without any shaving knowledge just wasn't something I was ready to do. I'd heard so many horror stories about shaving: the hairs will come back and they'll be even thicker and more numerous, the razor will tear your skin off, and so forth. In fact, I'd already shaved my hairy arms using my dad's razor. That wasn't the brightest idea, in hindsight, because the hairs grew back even thicker and darker and in a very odd pattern.

Back to Alice. One day, we were sitting next to each other during recess when out of the blue she pointed at my legs and jokingly said, "I'm going to buy you a shaving kit for your next birthday!" Wait, what? Was this well-meant or was she poking fun? I knew my leg hair was more visible than hers, but was it really *that* noticeable? I clearly had no clue. Notice how I'd never thought about shaving my legs until someone pointed out that they "needed" to be attended to.

Think about it: when did women decide to start getting rid of their body hair? And more important, when did it stop being a choice and start being a must?

First of all, growing body hair is a natural phenomenon for both men and women. Facial hair, armpit hair, leg hair, pubic hair, back hair . . . wherever you have skin, you can grow hair.

FRIDA KAHLO

Both boys and girls have facial hair. Usually, it is unnoticeable with girls. Teenage boys' facial hair becomes dark and thick under the influence of testosterone (that's the male sex hormone). Growing a beard is one of the effects of male hormones. So is noticeable facial hair something only boys have?

No. Girls can have visible facial hair, too. Some girls might have a little moustache or a

HARNAAM KAUR

slight unibrow, just like the famous Mexican painter Frida Kahlo.

Another example is Harnaam Kaur, who's had a full, glossy beard of her own since she was sixteen. This is a symptom of her PCOS (polycystic ovary syndrome), a condition that messes with a women's sex hormone (estrogen and progesterone) levels and throws them off balance. Common symptoms include hirutism, also known as hairiness.

For a very long time, Harnaam chose to go through the painful and tedious process of removing her facial hair, but that's how she allowed the bullies to get to her. She tried shaving, waxing, plucking—everything. She wanted so badly to be accepted by others when she hadn't fully accepted herself. With the help of her supportive brother, she slowly gained confidence. She finally let her beard grow. Just for a couple of days, at first. Then later, she stopped going to the beauty salon altogether and decided never to have *her* (she uses female pronouns to refer to her beard) removed ever again, even if she could!

The message Harnaam wants to spread is that women should do whatever they want with their body hair. If it makes you sad, remove it. If you like it, rock it!

So do you have to shave? To cut to the chase: no, you don't. But you may have noticed there are some prejudices out there about shaving, and different rules seem to apply for men and women. If you already have some experience with shaving, you might or might not have had an unpleasant, itchy burning on your skin, or maybe the areas you've shaved have felt very dry and sensitive at times. In this section, I'll explain what you can do to take care of your shaved skin and what to do when you accidentally cut yourself while shaving (because that can sting *real* bad!).

Shaving 101
Continued

When you're ready to start experimenting with hair removal, you'll notice there are tons of different methods to choose from. The most common ways of removing hair are: manual shaving with a razor, electric shaving, and waxing (or plucking if it's tiny, facial hair).

There are so many different brands of razors out there, but generally, the good old drugstore brands will definitely get the job done. Prices for manual razors range from real cheap ($2), which I don't recommend, to quite expensive ($20 to $30). The pricey ones aren't necessarily any better than their more affordable counterparts, so any razor that's bang in the middle of the price range will be perfectly fine. For electric razors, you'll pay a lot more ($50 to $200). Waxing strips are usually priced between $5 and $15, depending on the brand and the number of strips in the box.

Whatever method you choose, taking care of your skin after hair removal is extremely important. If you use a manual razor for shaving, you're going to have a rough time if you don't use shaving cream during and body lotion after running the razor over your skin. Red, itchy skin is not uncommon if you don't take proper care of the areas you shave. If you shave safely, however, you can easily achieve smooth, hairless skin with zero or minimal irritation. Here are some very quick tips that worked for me (and I have sensitive skin):

• A bit of trial and error will probably be needed to find the hair removal method that works best for you. I've tried waxing and threading (with a thread in a beauty salon), but in the end, regular shaving still works best for me. I use shaving cream for very sensitive skin types, a razor that I change every two weeks, and a moisturizer to hydrate my skin after shaving.

• Use a good shaving cream if you use a manual razor. Your skin can feel tight if you only use water. Shaving cream makes it much easier to move your razor across the skin surface, and it also helps to keep your skin hydrated.

- Be careful when you shave (even when you're in a hurry because you only have twenty minutes left to get ready for that party)! Razors are sharp, and if you are too enthusiastic with them, you might end up cutting yourself. If this happens, don't panic. It can sting like a mofo, and there might be what looks like a lot of blood. Rinse the cut with water and disinfect it once you're out of the shower or bath. It's best not to cover the cut with a Band-Aid, though; if you allow air to get to it, the cut will scab over and heal faster.
- Take care of your shaving zones, wherever they are. Keep the skin hydrated and use baby powder to treat any irritation you may have. Especially for your bikini line, baby powder or baby lotion can go a long way in treating mild shaving rashes or bumps.
- Leave plenty of time between two shaving sessions. If you shave too often, the hair *will* grow back very quickly and you may end up with ingrown hairs. Trust me: you don't want that.
- Drink enough water to keep your skin supple and healthy.

Remember that shaving is a choice, never a must.

Chapter Three

ON FOOD COMAS AND FOOD BABIES

Why is it so important to have a healthy relationship with food? Read on to find answers to some pressing and important food questions!

WHY UNHEALTHY FOODS ARE DELICIOUS . . . BUT SO BAD!

I enjoy a good bowl of pasta from time to time. I allow myself to have a nice dessert after dinner. I can't resist my favorite kind of chips, and I have a soda every now and then. I know that eating junk food regularly is linked to many health problems, such as heart diseases and high blood pressure. Then why do I keep doing this to myself? I know that with every bite of pizza and every sip of soda, I'm slowly killing myself, but I just find eating junk food *so* satisfying.

What is it that makes doughnuts, ice cream, chips, and pizza so delicious? And addictive? I often curse the unfairness of it all. I wish junk food was healthy and vegetables weren't.

Michael Moss is a *New York Times* journalist and the writer of *Salt, Sugar, Fat: How the Food Giants Hooked Us.* Steven Witherly is a food scientist who's spent the last twenty years looking for that one thing that makes certain foods tastier than others and has collected his findings in his report "Why Humans Like Junk Food." So it's safe to say that both men are junk-food experts.

According to Moss, junk food can be seen as a kind of legalized narcotic. The big fast-food companies have succeeded in manipulating three key ingredients to make these bad-for-you foods irresistable: salt, sugar, and fat. Those ingredients behave like drugs in our brain— they give us pleasure and satisfaction. And, of course, if we consume large amounts of those three substances, they'll always leave us craving more, simply to keep satisfying the high levels we've become accustomed to. Moss explains that the team of scientists employed by junk-food companies calculate precisely how much of each ingredient is needed to keep their consumers hooked. And they keep tweaking this secret formula to make their food even more addictive.

Whitherly, in his report, discusses the "Big Six," which are six factors that determine why certain foods are more delicious and addictive than others. Our favorite snacks usually show most, or all, of the following characteristics:

• **Taste Hedonics**, as Whitherly calls them. "Delicious" foods contain a lot of salt, sugar, MSG (flavor enhancers), and flavor-active compounds. The quantities are measured carefully to maximize psychological effects. Taste plays an important role in how much we enjoy certain foods, as well as other parameters such as temperature, texture, and fat percentage.

• **Dynamic Contrast.** The tastiest foods have contrasting textures and flavors. We like it when our foods crunch, snap, crackle, and pop. Along with food hedonics, this is the most important reason why we like certain foods better than others. Also, our food has to look good; we are visual creatures, after all.

- **Evoked Qualities.** Part of the reason why we like certain foods is that we remember how much we enjoyed eating them in the past. Thinking about it, we remember exactly what that meal tasted like, and so we're happy to discover that it's still just as yummy when we order it the next time. This kind of food nostalgia explains why the recipes to some classic foods and drinks, such as the Big Mac and Coca-Cola, have been the same for many years.
- **Food Pleasure Equation.** If a food or a drink has a low calorie count, the manufacturer has to add more bells and whistles to the recipe to increase the overall pleasure. Think about diet sodas: they have less sugar and calories, but if you read the label, you'll find a whole bunch of additives and extra stuff used to make it taste good.
- **Caloric Density.** If 0 is the score for water and 9 for pure fat, the sweet spot for junk food is somewhere around 4 to 5.
- **Emulsion Theory.** Our taste buds adore emulsions. We enjoy it when two liquids or substances that do not naturally mix are joined together. Salt-fat or sugar-fat combos especially are almost universally considered yummy.

All of these theories might seem a bit abstract to us, because most of the time we have absolutely no clue what's in our junk food. Bearing the Big Six in mind makes it a little easier to understand why we like, let's say, Doritos—a popular brand of tortilla chips that brings a lot of pleasure to a lot of people. The chips combine high quantities of salt with high quantities of sugar. That's right, sugar. Even though we don't really notice it, it's there, and it's what gives the chips their signature flavor. The seasoning gives them an extra kick and increases salivation. The tortilla chips are crispy and crunchy, and the evoked qualities are enhanced. Whenever you buy your favorite kind of Doritos, they taste exactly the same as they did the last time—that's why they're never *not* good.

So, yes, there are scientific reasons that explain why your brain likes junk food: big brands have succeeded in creating a perfect balance between sweet and savory that your brain just love love loves. Food companies spend millions and millions of dollars to design the kind of foods that get you hooked.

Luckily for us, we can conquer this addiction. Obviously, it's nothing like being addicted to a hard drug, but some people do experience a really strong urge to consume these processed foods that is almost like a drug addict's yearning for the next hit. Certain people simply have a stronger hedonic drive for junk food than others. In addition to psychical reasons, there are a number of psychological reasons why people might crave junk food, for example, stress or emotional eating.

The question is: can we kick the habit and beat this addiction on our own? The answer is yes. If you eat less junk food, you'll crave less junk food. Unfortunately, it's not always that simple. "Just stop doing it" is the theoretical solution to any kind of addiction, but the reality is a little more complicated. Here are some practical suggestions to help you break the fast-food eating cycle:

• If you don't keep junk food around the house, you can't eat it. My lifestyle and health coach, Amy, tells me that when I go grocery shopping, I should try to stay in the outer aisles of the supermarket.

Why? Because that's where the vegetables, fruits, and other healthy foods tend to be. The deeper you go into a grocery store, the more processed foods you'll find.

• My grandma once told me: if you can't pronounce the ingredients, don't buy it. By that she meant stearing clear of all the chemicals that are added for flavor or the preservatives that help keep the food edible for a long time.

• Experiment with cooking. You can find lots of delicious and easy recipes on Pinterest, even weekly menus! Try new things and mix up your meals to keep things interesting.

• Avoid stress-eating. I know, I shouldn't be talking. I often make this mistake myself. But recently, I've managed to find other ways of coping with my stress. We all have stress sometimes, but there are other, healthier ways to reduce it. You could try breathing exercises or yoga. Going for a run, listening to music, or creating art are really good options, too.

• Remember that each day is a new day. Okay, so maybe you overdid it a little on the ice cream and pizza yesterday, but that doesn't mean you can't try again today. Every day is a new opportunity to take better care of yourself.

There's a lot more to be said about (junk) food, so if you're interested, here are some great documentaries on this topic. Because we all love food and we all love movies, right?

• *Cowspiracy: The Sustainability Secret* (2014): explores the claim that animal agriculture is the number-one threat to the environment nowadays.

• *Food, Inc.* (2008): deals with the issue of corporate farming in America.

• *Soul Food Junkies* (2012): positions the cultural implications of African American soul food against their healthfulness.

• *Super Size Me* (2004): about a guy who eats nothing but McDonald's, three times a day, for an entire month.

• *Hungry for Change* (2012): claims to reveal all the secrets the diet industry is keeping from you.

25 SLICES OF BACON

= 3 DONUTS

= 3.5 BAGELS

6.6 POUNDS (3KG) OF CARROTS =

(JUST A LOT OF CARROTS)

= 2 BIG MACs

WHAT DOES 1000 CAL LOOK LIKE ???

= 1 MILKSHAKE + WHIPPED CREAM (24OZ)

= 2 LARGE GLASSES OF ORANGE JUICE

ONE 14" PIZZA REGULAR CRUST =

= 142 ALMONDS

= 21 CHICKEN NUGGETS

= 10 BANANAS

WHY DRINKING WATER CAN CHANGE YOUR LIFE

You probably already know that your body mostly consists of water: about 60 percent. On average, we lose one to two liters of water a day from breathing alone. Sweating and urinating also cause us to lose a lot of water. All that water has to come from somewhere—that's why we have to, you've guessed it, drink it!

If you don't drink enough, your body will become dehydrated. When this happens, your cells run dry and have a hard time taking care of the daily routines of your body. If you're thirsty, it's actually already too late. You should avoid getting thirsty by proactively drinking enough water during the day. You can do that by taking a water bottle with you to school, work, or the gym. You'll be sipping more water and you won't even know you're doing it. Obviously, you'll have to pee more often, but that's just how your body works, and you'll get used to it eventually.

If you're fully hydrated, which is good, your pee should be color-less. If you're somewhat hydrated, your pee might be a bit yellowish. If your pee is a really dark shade of yellow, it means your body is severely dehydrated. What's the big deal, you're wondering? Well, since water is a very important fluid in your body (it helps to transport nutrients, keeps your muscles flexible, speeds up the healing process when you're sick, etc.), it needs to be replenished and refreshed from time to time. If not, your skin will get dry, you'll feel tired and low on energy, you'll get headaches, and you could experience a whole range of other health problems.

Every health website or magazine will probably tell you something different about the amount of water you should drink. Some will claim 33 ounces (1 liter) is enough, while others will insist that 67 ounces (2 liters) is nowhere near enough. The truth is, every person has different needs. For example, if you're an athlete, you probably need to drink more water than the average person. You can find out how much water you need on a normal day by dividing your weight (in pounds) by two (result in ounces). For example: I weigh 132 pounds. 132 divided by 2 is 66 ounces. That's approximately 1.95 liters (or about 8 cups) of water a day. Of course, on days when I exercise or it's hot outside, I'll need to drink additional cups in order to stay hydrated.

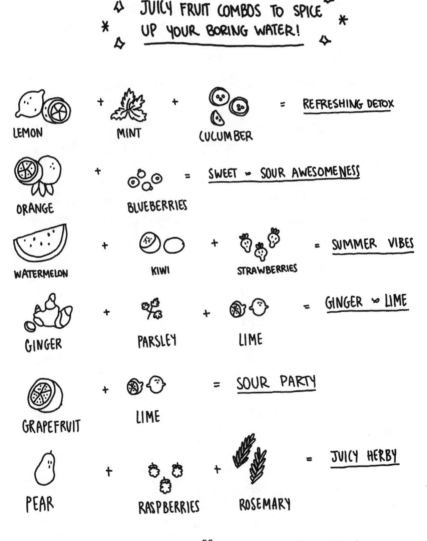

JUICY FRUIT COMBOS TO SPICE UP YOUR BORING WATER!

LEMON + MINT + CUCUMBER = REFRESHING DETOX

ORANGE + BLUEBERRIES = SWEET ~ SOUR AWESOMENESS

WATERMELON + KIWI + STRAWBERRIES = SUMMER VIBES

GINGER + PARSLEY + LIME = GINGER ~ LIME

GRAPEFRUIT + LIME = SOUR PARTY

PEAR + RASPBERRIES + ROSEMARY = JUICY HERBY

Coffee and Tea Are Not Substitutes for Water!

Yes, coffee and tea contain water. However, caffeinated drinks also flush the water out of your system. So don't count on them alone to keep you hydrated. Avoid drinks like sodas and soft drinks, because they contain a lot of sugar and artificial flavors that are really bad for you. The best option is just to drink plain water.

You think it's boring? It doesn't have to be!

Here's how to pimp your basic water:

- Buy a hipster water bottle that will motivate you to drink water.
- If you like it fresh, add some lemon, lime, and mint to your water bottle.
- If you like it fruity, try a combo of strawberries, raspberries, and blueberries. For extra flavor, gently squeeze the fruits before you add them to your water.
- Strawberry, watermelon, and kiwi are your best friends! Simply add them to your water to give that detox boost your body deserves.
- Experiment with combos of flavors: grapefruit and thyme, pineapple and rosemary, cucumber and lemon . . . or simply create your own.

IT'S COOL TO STAY HYDRATED

You can start your morning the right way: while you were sleeping, a lot of toxins and waste products have built up overnight and your body has become super dehydrated. As soon as you wake up, drink a large cup of water just to kick-start your metabolism and to get your blood flowing. Do the same thing before you go to bed. The water will help your body detox during the night.

Take water breaks during the day. Get up from your desk or sofa and get a glass of water, or sip regularly from your water bottle. Drink water before and after you eat, approximately thirty minutes before and thirty minutes after every meal. This helps your digestive system process your food.

Also, keep an eye on your skin and body. You can often tell from your skin if your body needs more water or not. If you don't drink enough, your skin can lose elasticity and appear more wrinkly than it actually is. Your skin is your biggest organ, so you better take good care of it.

When you exercise, always keep water close. Drink before, during, and after every workout—it's recommended to take a few sips at least every twenty minutes or so. Remember to keep your water and sodium (salt) intake balanced.

Eat more fruits and veggies! Boring? Maybe. Hydrating? Sure! Watermelon, strawberries, tomatoes, cucumbers, broccoli, peppers, cauliflower, and grapefruit are examples of juicy foods that contain more than 90 percent water. And getting water this way is fun, because you don't have to drink it.

Avoid drinking a lot of alcohol (and only if you are of legal age, of course). You might feel like you're hydrating by doing so, but that's mostly because the alcohol disturbs the communication between your kidneys and your brain. In other words: when you drink alcohol, your body "forgets" to tell you that it needs water, which can result in dehydration.

Drinking *too much* water is also a thing, and it's called hyponatremia. It can be dangerous. If your cells have to absorb too much excess water, they start to swell up. If your brain cells are swollen, that can cause a lot of health problems, such as confusion, disorientation, nausea, cramps, bad headaches, and even coma. Hyponatremia has killed a number of marathon runners in the past.

So, always keep a healthy balance, peeps! The trick is not to wait until you're thirsty and to make sure you drink enough, but don't overdo your water intake, either.

SUGAR COMA: HOW SWEETS CAN MAKE YOU FEEL BAD

It's strange, right? Eating sugar, which should give you an energy boost right away, can actually make you feel lazy or tired in the end. You might be energetic or hyper for a while, but as soon as the sugar buzz wears off, you'll start feeling sluggish and sleepy. There are many reasons that explain why you feel this way, but it usually has something to do with your blood-sugar level. When you eat or drink something sugary, this causes a sudden spike in your blood-sugar level, and your body then needs to recover and adjust to this sudden change.

If you often feel really tired after consuming sugary goods, you should consult your doctor to check for sugar-related conditions like diabetes. However, if it only happens once in a while, you shouldn't be worried, because this is normal for many people.

Your body works hard to balance your sugar levels, and this takes a lot of energy under any circumstances. If you add overly sugary foods to the mix, your body has to work extra hard to maintain the status quo. As a counterreaction, it releases a hormone called insulin to gradually lower the blood-sugar level. This is when you can feel your energy levels plummet and you become tired or lazy.

Sounds familiar? Then maybe you should take a close look at your sugar intake. Consider the following foods. Do you recognize a lot of stuff you've been eating recently?

• Cake, chocolates, candy, pastries, anything confectionery
• Fruit (bananas, grapes, apples, pineapple) but also fruit and vegetable juices
• Pizza, potatoes, chips, and pasta. You might not expect this, but processed foods contain a lot of artificial sweeteners that can make you feel dizzy and tired. The body treats those sugars like any other kind of sugar.
• Dairy products (e.g., milk, yogurt)
• Corn products (e.g., popcorn, cornbread)

Giving Up Sugar?—
That's the Question

Hold on, sister! One step at a time. If you're used to having sugar e
very day (from fruit, desserts, junk food, or other foods), it's not
recommended to completely remove it from your diet all of the
sudden. Even if giving up sugar is a long-term goal you've set for
yourself, do it in baby steps so your body can get used to the change.
However, I suggest you consult with a professional first before you
take any action. If you want to keep your energy level up, it's best
to avoid drastic changes to your eating patterns (such as crash diets),
so your blood-sugar levels remain stable.

How Not to Feel Tired
After Eating Sugary Foods

There's a number of things you can do. First of all, drink plenty of
water to keep your body cells working. Dehydration can lead to
tiredness, as explained previously. Eat smaller meals, and eat more
frequently. If possible, eat your meals around the same time every day.
If you eat more frequently, but smaller amounts, it's easier for your
digestive system to process your food. Less energy used = less tired.

Eat more foods that are high in fiber (beans, nuts, blackberries)
and fewer foods that are high in carbohydrates (white bread, white
rice). My health coach taught me that fibrous foods keep you satisfied
for longer, so you'll have fewer cravings after or between your meals.

Another great way to prevent fatigue after sugar intake is to
exercise. Exercising for twenty minutes, three times a week, will
increase your productivity and energy levels while reducing your
stress levels.

I took the test myself and reduced my sugar intake for one whole
week. In my experience, one week was too short to really feel the
difference—you'll probably be able to notice the first real effects
after two or three weeks. My findings, though, were as follows:

- Surprisingly, I felt more energetic in the morning, and I am the laziest person in the whole country in the morning hours. I usually lie around stinking in my bed for about an hour before I finally manage to get up. To my own surprise, after two or three days of eating less sugar, I found myself jumping out of bed right as the alarm sounded.
- I did get crankier and fussier—especially during the first days. My mood swings were more intense than usual, but I'm not sure if that was only because of the lack of sugar.
- My sugar cravings were crazy in the beginning, but I conquered them after only a week. Instead of mindlessly snacking on junk, I grabbed a handful of nuts or some rice crackers when I felt hungry.
- Normally, I drink my tea with a teaspoon of agave syrup. Although that's a natural sweetener, I gave it up, too. In the beginning, I disliked the pure taste of the tea. I soon realized why: I'd become addicted to the fake sweet taste of my favorite hot beverage. I switched to forest fruit tea for that week, because it's naturally sweeter and doesn't require any additional sugar to be tasty.
- I couldn't stop eating the natural sugars that are found in fruits. I felt like I was allowed to keep *something* sweet in my diet, so I kept eating fruit, mostly bananas and apples.
- My stomach felt less bloated.

In general, I didn't experience that much of a difference in my one-week trial: my skin stayed the same and I didn't lose any weight. Not that that was my intention, but I kind of expected it to happen.

Regardless, trying to reduce your sugar intake will certainly benefit your health. I'm not saying you should completely cut out sugar, because 1) removing all sugars from your diet is really difficult, as sugar is almost everywhere, and 2) you should discuss the implications of any diet with your doctor first to make sure you are approaching such an eating change healthily.

YOU SHOULD EAT BREAKFAST!

Why do you need breakfast? People always say that breakfast is the most important meal of the day. Well, it's true. It's easy to skip breakfast, or to think that you're not hungry in the morning, but let me tell you why you should have a good, solid breakfast every day:

1. Breakfast is the best way to recharge your batteries. Whole-grain bread, oatmeal, and fruit are an easy way to get energy-boosting nutrients into your system. Eating breakfast means saying good-bye to sleepiness in class.
2. Breakfast will help you concentrate better. Your brain needs fuel, too, as it's been very active during the night. If you want to learn something in class and actually remember it later, having breakfast will improve your alertness and memory.
3. Breakfast will help you maintain a healthy weight. Yes, I used to think that skipping breakfast was a way to limit my calories, but this is a huge misunderstanding. If you don't have a nutritious breakfast, you'll be craving more quick snacks during the day, which can have a negative impact on your weight and overall health.
4. Even if you don't feel hungry, breakfast can be super delish. There are endless tasty options and recipes (try banana pancakes or quick wraps) other than boring and unhealthy cereal to eat in the morning. You can prepare your breakfast before you go to bed, so the only thing you have to do in the morning is grab it from the fridge!

EASY AND GREAT WAYS TO EAT BREAKFAST

We've all been there: you're running late for school, you're hungry and half-dressed and crazy stressed because you haven't packed your bag yet. Your mom is telling you to eat your breakfast first, because that's important. "No time!" you yell as you run out the door and start chasing after your school bus.

Okay, so you didn't have breakfast, you can't concentrate in class, and you feel like you might pass out soon. Your body is running on its last drops of fuel, and you feel super dizzy and cranky all day. Not too much fun, is it?

Let's rewind a couple hours and take a look at a scenario in which you actually make time for breakfast. I'm not suggesting you devour a complete Sunday brunch when your time is limited and you have to get ready for school, but there are some quick, easy, and delicious options that will get the job done.

Don't believe me? Try some of these recipes and you'll be shocked:

EASY BREAKFAST YOGURT
4 mins

Greek yogurt, plain yogurt, or any kind of yogurt you like
Honey or agave syrup

Your favorite kind of jam
Chopped almonds or other nuts

Take a bowl and add all the ingredients, placing the jam and nuts on top.

EXPRESS OATMEAL
4-5 mins

Instant oatmeal
Skim milk or almond milk

Fresh berries
Cocoa powder (or cinnamon)

Microwave the oatmeal and milk in a bowl for about two minutes. Add the berries and sprinkle some cocoa powder (or cinnamon) on top for extra flavor.

FRUIT CROSTINI
4 mins

Baguette, sliced

Ricotta cheese

Honey

Sliced strawberries

Mix the ricotta and honey. Spread the honey on the pieces of baguette. Add the sliced strawberries on top.

WHOLE GRAIN PORRIDGE
10 hours + 10 mins

1½ cups water

¾ cup oats

¾ cup barley

3 tbsp brown sugar

½ cup cornmeal

1 tbsp vanilla extract (optional)

A pinch of kosher salt

1 tbsp cinnamon

Add the water, oats, barley, brown sugar, cornmeal, vanilla (optional), salt, and cinnamon in a slow cooker. Leave it to soak overnight. In the morning, place the cooker on high heat and cook until soft. Pour it in a bowl and top with your favorite nuts or fruit.

SMOKED SALMON BAGEL
3 mins

Bagel, split

Cream cheese

Smoked salmon, in slices

A bit of chopped parsley

A bit of chopped chives

Kosher salt & pepper

Toast the bagel. Spread some cream cheese on it, add the salmon slices, and season with the herbs and spices.

If you still think you don't have enough time to prepare any of these in the morning, make something that you can eat on the go, like a wrap, smoothie, or sandwich. Also, take some fruit with you, like an apple, banana, or pear.

+ DELICIOUS SNACKS ON THE GO:

NUT MIX

CUCUMBER/CARROT STICKS WITH HUMMUS

HARD-BOILED EGG

LOW-SALT POPCORN

GRANOLA BAR

YOU CANNOT SURVIVE ON RAMEN NOODLES ALONE (I'M SO SORRY)

I remember having a lot of ramen noodles as a kid, because my Asian mom would often prepare them as a quick snack or a light meal. The way she cooked the instant ramen got me hooked. She didn't just pour water over them and let them soak for a minute; no, she literally cooked them, then stir-fried them in a wok, added veggies, chicken, or beef, and used her own spices instead of the flavor package that came with the noodles. After tasting my mom's special ramen noodles, I never wanted to have anything else in my life ever again.

I honestly thought ramen noodles were the best thing ever, but it never crossed my mind that living on noodles alone might be super unhealthy. Let's take a look at what *could* happen if you did.

There's this girl in the UK named Georgi Readman, who's been eating just ramen noodles for more than thirteen years, and she isn't planning on changing that anytime soon. As a reason for this weird diet, Georgi claims that she can't stand the texture of fruits, veggies, or any other type of food. Thoughts of other foods make her sick. But ramen noodles don't bother her. So that's what she eats.

As a result, Georgi can't meet her friends for dinner unless there's noodles on the menu. She even freaks out if something else comes into contact with the noodles she's eating.

Another story stars Kieran Dooley, who was inspired by the movie *Super Size Me*, and who tried to live off ramen noodles for a month and got totally sick as a result. His challenge was to eat nothing but three packs of instant noodles a day. As a student, he'd already gone through a phase when he ate them every day, so he didn't think it would be that difficult.

He tried to keep the experiment interesting by choosing different flavors. But when he studied the nutrition label on the packages, he noticed something alarming: each pack contained about 1,300 milligrams of sodium (it's recommended to limit your salt intake to 2,300 milligrams a day). Too much sodium increases your risk of suffering strokes, heart attacks, and high blood pressure. But the sodium was not the only problem Dooley had to deal with. Some days, he wasn't even able to finish his three packs because he was so nauseated.

By the end of the challenge, he'd lost an unhealthy twenty-four pounds (approximately eleven kilos), and he felt lethargic and sick to his stomach all the time. Apart from the physical effects, he also became extremely moody and cranky.

Dooley wouldn't want to repeat the noodle diet ever again. "It was hell, but it was worth it, in the name of science," he concludes.

IT HAS COME TO PASS, GEORGI STARTED DREAMING SHE HAD EATEN ALL THE RAMEN IN THE WORLD AND THERE WOULD BE NOTHING LEFT TO EAT...

What both stories teach us is that living solely off a product that is basically a salty snack is not a healthy way to live. Doctors say that Georgi is malnourished and that she has the health of an eighty-year-old, when she's only eighteen years old. The key is to stick to a balanced diet that provides enough vitamins.

MY PEERS KEEP TELLING ME, "YOU SHOULDN'T BE EATING THAT!"

Whenever I'm lazing on the couch with some friends, and I'm devouring my favorite kind of chips, there's always at least one person who just *has* to tell me that "chips aren't healthy." I often pretend I don't hear the comment, and I usually continue to enjoy my snack. But then, suddenly, the guilt kicks in. *I shouldn't have been eating this* . . . and I start to feel really bad about myself. And then there's the times when I go out with my friends and we find ourselves craving a midnight snack after we're done partying. I feel doubly guilty when I'm the only one in the group having a midnight snack. Most of my friends wouldn't dream of telling me to resist my late-night cravings, but I can sense their judging eyes staring at me every time I'm devouring a cheesy garlic bread by myself.

I remember this one time I had a friend over my house, and she was obsessed with losing weight. That's fine—that's what she was into—but often she would shame other people for eating the stuff she wouldn't eat. She probably didn't even realize that she was doing it, but she was. So this one particular night, we were having mac and cheese for dinner, and she left the cheesy crust on the side of her plate. After we were done eating, I asked if she was going to finish that cheesy crust (some people save it for last, because it's just the best part), and she got all angry with me, claiming that I was trying to make her fat. I wasn't. I was simply trying to find out if she still wanted the cheesy crust or not, because if she didn't, I wanted to finish it. The comment she made, however, sent me straight into guilt-trip mode and made me question my eating habits. So no, I didn't take her cheesy crust in the end and I felt extra bad about having wanted to eat it in the first place.

I'm a girl who loves good, greasy food, and I know I'm not the only one. I enjoy a good mac and cheese, fries, pizza, and pasta. And I would never tell anyone that they shouldn't enjoy those things. That's because I hate it when other people do it to me. Trying to go all health-coach style on me and telling me what I should and shouldn't eat . . . Gah! That's why I won't do it to you, either. The choice of what you put into your mouth is completely yours; all I'll do is provide a few healthier alternatives.

I try to promote a healthy relationship with food, and I don't think you should feel bad or curse yourself for having something unhealthy from time to time. At the same time, I'm also here to tell you that you don't *have* to eat a bag of chips if you *don't* want to. If clean eating is your thing, I salute you. But again, finding the right balance is key, even when you're eating healthy.

FOOD NEVER DISAPPOINTS ME.

It might not be my place to tell you what you should or shouldn't be eating, but I can tell you what I have stopped eating or drinking since I was a teenager. Not because I don't like the taste (because in most cases I still do), but because what I was eating was pretty unhealthy for *my* body. Let's take a look at the stuff I stopped eating and drinking after high school. Consider this list just a suggestion of what you could possibly reduce in your diet to make your eating choices a little healthier:

- **Energy drinks.** All types, all flavors—I drank them all. Not only at times when I was cramming for a test or an exam, but throughout any regular day: when I woke up or when I was hanging around at home. I drank about 33 ounces of energy drinks a day. Take it from me, the momentary buzz is not worth the seriously harmful effects on your body. I stopped drinking energy drinks and switched to coffee to still get that caffeine jolt, but I never have more than one cup of coffee a day, either.

- **White bread.** I loved white bread as a teenager, because I hated the taste of the seeds in whole-grain bread. All good, nutritious elements are omitted from white bread, making it virtually worthless nutrition-wise. I taught myself to get used to whole-wheat bread, and I find it delicious now.

- **Diet sodas.** I got rid of these, as they contain a ton of sweeteners and artificial flavors. So I steer clear of them nowadays. When I do drink soda, I just go for the regular kind and skip the diet.

Notice how quite a few junk food items seem to be missing from the list? Well, that's because I still eat or drink them. However, I don't do so every day and not even every week. I try to keep a balance between clean food and junk food, and I also try not to worry about judgmental friends who may have a different view of eating these types of foods.

TO MEAT OR NOT TO MEAT?

Perhaps you've considered becoming a vegetarian (meaning you stop consuming meat and fish) or even a vegan (meaning you stop consuming all meat, as well as other foods that are processed using animal products, like milk, eggs, butter, and so forth). Maybe you're a vegetarian or a vegan already, in which case most of what comes next won't be news to you. If you are thinking about becoming a

herbivore, continue to read all about my experiences with meat
and vegetarianism.

About 200,000 years ago, the human species started to evolve,
especially when it came to how they consumed their food. They
discovered that cooking their foods made them easier to digest.
As a long-term result over many, many generations, the human
digestive system became smaller, because it didn't have to work as
hard as it did before.

Our ancestors' diet consisted mainly of vegetables, supplemented
by a bit of meat. The smarter humans became, the bigger their
brains grew and the more energy they required, so they learned how
to hunt and kill animals more efficiently — to feed their growing brains.
Wherever tribes of humans migrated, many of their preferred prey
animals soon became extinct. (That should give you an idea of how
much meat they consumed.) They killed so many animals for meat that
they were eventually forced into agriculture to avoid starving
to death.

So, yes, meat was a *very* big deal to our ancestors, but the human
race has evolved some more since then. These days, we no longer
need to hunt or eat lots of meat just to make it through winter.
Today, vegetarians are generally just as healthy as meat-eaters, and
they are less likely to suffer from heart diseases.

Carnivore or Vegetarian?
The Conundrum

Meat has the perfect taste combination that gets many people hooked:
umami mixed with salt and the taste of grilled fat. Basically, you can
get addicted to meat. But does that mean we actually *need* it?

No, we don't. We have a wide range of alternative sources that
can provide the protein and vitamins our body needs. Choosing to eat
more consciously can save your health, millions of animals, and the
environment. Cutting meat from your diet helps the environment *a lot
more* than using less water or saving on electricity.

Did you know that the production of one burger uses just as much water as a hundred *days* of showering? Me neither. Or that ten pounds of grain (4.5 kilos) is needed to produce a single pound of beef? Every day, we clear huge patches of rain forest to build farms in order to sustain our meat addiction. Long story short: the meat industry is the number-one climate killer.

If we take a look at how, let's say, eggs and milk are produced, we have to face the fact that those products generally don't come from bio farms where animals have a great life. No, in almost 100 percent of all cases, our eggs and milk come from intensive livestock farming, where animals are treated like sh*t. They are kept in the smallest cages possible, so that farmers can make as much money as possible.

Baby piglets are castrated at a very young age, chickens have their beaks cut off, and animals are slaughtered alive without any kind of anaesthetic. So, if we continue to buy animal products that are the result of such terrible practices, we are basically financing this kind of cruelty.

Despite all the horror that goes on behind the scenes, advertisements insist that we *need* animal products to keep a balanced diet. How many of us *didn't* grow up hearing that drinking milk would make our bones stronger? That's bullsh*t, by the way. Almost all of the nutrients we need for building strong bones can be found in higher concentrations in plant-based alternatives. You'll only need to find an alternative source of vitamin B12, since this vitamin doesn't naturally occur in vegetables.

It takes a lot of courage to admit that eating meat is wrong, but, in fact, you can already make a change by understanding and acknowledging that animal cruelty is wrong and should be stopped. Before I started doing research on the topic for this book, I was already trying to take small steps and giving up one animal product at a time. These were some super-easy things I started doing, almost subconsciously, and they've been part of my daily life ever since:

- Drinking almond or coconut milk instead of cows' milk.
- Sweetening with agave syrup instead of honey.
- Introducing at least one or two vegetarian-only days each week.
- Eating soy-based yogurt instead of regular yogurt.
- Choosing a vegetarian dish when ordering at a restaurant.
- Buying vegan cheese.

These simple steps have really helped me on my way toward a healthier and cruelty-free lifestyle. In time, it would be awesome if I could avoid all animal products I come across on a daily basis. But, as with any drastic changes in your diet, it's not the best idea to over-haul everything overnight. First things first: I gradually cut out red meat, and honestly? I haven't craved a steak in over a year now.

In Belgium, an annual campaign called "Days Without Meat" challenges people to give up meat for forty days. This vegetarian initiative has gained a lot of popularity in the past couple of years, and it's become a yearly tradition that challenges meat-eaters to discover how diverse and delicious veggie life can be. I used to be one of those meat-eaters, and I was super proud when I completed the challenge. I have to admit that it wasn't always easy. Perhaps because I went cold turkey (pun intended); I stopped eating meat from one day to the next without any steady decrease or preparation. But by the time the challenge neared its conclusion, I found myself experimenting with tons of new plant-based recipes, and I have to admit I had a lot of fun discovering new tastes and flavors.

If you're thinking about giving vegetarianism a try, but you're worried you'll have uncontrollable meat cravings, have no fear. You can trick your mind into thinking you're eating meat when you're actually eating veggies or other substitute products. Forget about the myth that vegetarians only eat tofu and kale—it's outdated and ridiculous. Being a vegetarian is certainly not boring!

But . . . Cheese!

That's true: cheese is made from milk and milk comes from cows, goats, and other animals. If you give up meat (on some days), you're already on the right track. If you want to take your cruelty-free diet to the next level, you can switch to vegan cheese. I promise there are plenty of different kinds out there, and I can assure you that they taste the same as regular cheese, minus the guilt!

The Costs of the Veggie Life

You're right that some processed vegetarian meat substitutes are pricey. But those things aren't always the healthiest options, either. Like other processed foods, they contain a lot of salt, so they're not always as good for you as you might think. Foods such as vegetables, fruits, nuts, seitan, tempeh, and quinoa are much better alternatives, and they don't have to be expensive, especially if you buy them locally.

Some of the worst things you can eat as a vegetarian are:

- **Veggie burgers and meatless chicken nuggets** — they contain a *lot* of sodium.
- **Artificially sweetened protein powders** — you don't want this to be your primary source of protein. Instead, choose products that contain natural ingredients.
- **Salted nuts** — these have too much sugar and salt, which means you're losing all the benefits.
- **Mock meats** — they are typically high in sodium and they're still processed.
- **Anything fried** — if you chose the veggie option of spring rolls, for example, that's okay. You can have it from time to time, but don't overdo it. Eating fried vegetarian stuff is no better for your health than eating fried meat.

Plan your meals ahead, preferably for the whole week. This can actually save you a lot of time and money. The veggies you buy can be used in multiple meals during the week. For example, if you're cooking a homemade veggie tomato pasta on Monday, you can save the sauce that's leftover and use it as a burrito dip later that week. The options are endless and really fun. Cooking can be therapeutic, and if you cook your own meals from scratch, you'll experience a great sense of accomplishment and increase your healthy-food intake.

How to Deal with a Carnivorous Family

I know it can be difficult to persuade your parents to do something that's completely new to them. Perhaps your family has been used to eating meat for decades and a collective change might require some more motivation. A first step toward getting them on board is to openly tell them that you're trying to change your diet. That can be enough to convince your family to cook different things for you.

I had a hard time persuading my family to eat healthy and green, even for just a week. Unfortunately, they're still not enthusiastic about doing so, but that doesn't keep me from doing my thing.

Some practical tips to gradually change your family's diet:

- Begin by telling them about what you're trying to do. Have a conversation about how important it is to have a balanced diet—for the environment, for society, and for your personal overall health.
- Prove that eating green doesn't have to be boring. Even better: cook a nice meal for your family and invite them to discover something amazing they may never have tried.
- Even if you can't convince them to eat green every day, you can at least try to have a veggie night once a week. Let them get used to the idea. People are creatures of habit, and as soon as they adapt to any kind of vegetarian routine, they'll be more open to the whole idea.
- Remember that not having meat isn't the problem; it's the will to change a deeply rooted habit. Give them the meat facts regularly so they'll remember why they're doing this again.
- Don't expect a sudden change if they aren't ready yet. Changing something takes time, encouragement, motivation, and dedication.

So yes, it is pretty healthy to stop eating meat. Not only will it improve your health, but it'll also reduce your carbon footprint. Make sure that you're getting all the nutrients your body needs and adjust your food intake accordingly. There are a bunch of creative recipe ideas that taste even better than your old faithful beef cheeseburger. The options are practically limitless. If you're looking for veggie/vegan inspiration, make sure to check out:

- onegreenplanet.org and ecowatch.com
- Pinterest for super quick and easy inspiration. Also ideal for girls on a budget!
- Instagram accounts to give a quick follow for delicious ideas: @brusselsvegan, @mynewroots, @loveandlemons, @gkstories, @lifeofavegetarian, to name a few
- Awesome recipe books like *Vegan: The Cookbook* by Jean-Christian Jury, *Love Real Food* by Kathryne Taylor, *Bowls of Goodness* by Nina Olsson, *The New Vegetarian Cooking for Everyone* by Deborah Madison, and *On Vegetables* by Jeremy Fox

Chapter Four

FASHION NO-NO OR FASHION GURU?

F ashion queen or fashion noob? Let's be honest, who has a unique style at the age of twelve? Well, I sure didn't. Read all about creating your personal look, some easy DIYs, finding the right bra, and more!

CREATING YOUR OWN STYLE VS. FASHION TRENDS

If there's one thing in life that literally has zero rules to it, it's fashion. What people consider fashionable is very subjective, however, and it's all a matter of taste. As a matter of fact, you can wear whatever you want! How cool is that?

Before we dig deeper into the world of fashion, here are some quick tips on how to find your own style without wasting buckets full of money on clothes:

1. I previously talked about body shapes. You can save yourself a lot of time, money, and frustration by looking for pieces that fit your body type. Why? Because wearing clothes that are cool *and* comfortable is a win-win. You'll feel extra confident if you're comfortable in what you wear, and finding stylish cuts designed to fit your body shape is a good first step in that direction.

2. Instead of focusing on trends and replacing your entire wardrobe every season, it's a good idea to invest in a number of basics (you only need like ten) that you can combine with more trendy items or statement pieces that are *totally* you. The wonderful thing about basics is that they are pretty much timeless and allow for endless mixing and matching.

3. If you have too many clothes and want to downsize your wardrobe, here's a tip: ignore the little voice in your head that whispers, "I might still wear this" every time you pick up an item that hasn't seen the outside of your closet in forever. If you haven't worn a piece in the last year, you'll probably never wear it again and won't miss it when it's gone. And remember: it's a lot easier to compose an outfit if you have limited options. Donate the clothes you no longer need to a charity or sell them, but don't throw them away! You could make someone very happy with your lightly worn clothes.

4. If you're a fan of black clothes like me, consider wearing other colors once in a while. You'll be surprised how much easier it is to find nice pieces. Don't feel comfortable in brightly colored outfits just yet? Try them on in a clothing store without actually buying them. That's how you can get used to the image of you in something other than black.

5. Relax. Fashion is a language, not a science. Fashion mistakes are there to be made, so don't be afraid to get it wrong a couple of times before you find the right balance between *slayage* and comfort. Creating your own style doesn't happen overnight.

The difference between style and trends is that style never fades, while trends are temporary. Keeping up with every trend out there is exhausting, not to mention expensive. If you follow each trend, your closet will burst sooner or later. Unlike your wallet.

There's more to style than finding the right clothes and accessories. It's an attitude, and it's the way you rock your looks and show your confidence. It reflects how you perceive yourself, as a fierce young lady who is owning it!

Still looking for style ideas to create your own personal look? YouTube, Instagram, Pinterest, and lookbooks are endless sources of #inspiration!

Foolproof Hairstyles for Different Hair Types

We all want to wear our hair out of the way sometimes. Special thanks goes to my friends who have different hair types than I do and who added their faves.

ACTUAL EASY HAIRSTYLES

THAT YOU CAN TRY ON YOU OR YOUR FRIENDS!

① SPACE BUNS

- BRUSH EVERYTHING OUT
- SPLIT YOUR HAIR IN HALF
- TIE EACH SIDE IN A BUN
- PULL OUT SOME HAIRS FOR A MESSIER LOOK
- SPRAY SOME DRYSHAMPOO/HAIR SPRAY TO FINISH THE LOOK

② HEAD SCARF/BANDANA

- PICK A SCARF OF YOUR CHOICE
- WRAP IT AROUND YOUR HEAD OR TIE YOUR HAIR FIRST
- MAKE A KNOT AT THE BACK OF YOUR HEAD
- SECURE WITH A BOBBY PIN ON EACH SIDE

③ MESSY TOP BUN (WORKS BEST WITH UNWASHED HAIR)

- TAKE ALL OF YOUR HAIR, TIE IT IN A BUN
- WITH YOUR HANDS, LOOSEN EVERYTHING UP A BIT
- PULL OUT SOME HAIR FOR A MESSIER LOOK
- MAKE IT MORE CASUAL WITH SEA SALT SPRAY

④ BEDHEAD BEACH WAVES (HEATLESS)

- BEFORE YOU GO TO BED, TIE YOUR HAIR IN LIL' BUNS
- THE NEXT MORNING, RELEASE THE BUNS & SHAKE
- SEA SALT SPRAY/HAIR SPRAY HELPS TO ACHIEVE AND KEEP THE BEACHY LOOK

⑤ HALF UP HALF DOWN

- BRUSH OUT YOUR HAIR
- TAKE A FEW PIECES OF YOUR HAIR, PUT IT IN A BUN
- LEAVE THE REST OUT
- GREAT IF YOUR HAIR IS GREASY BUT YOU WANT TO WAIT AN EXTRA DAY

⑥ SHORT HAIR

- WAKE UP

Nine Life-Saving Makeup Hacks

Being a broke college student, I love collecting all kinds of tips that save me money and effort. Let's take a look at the following cheap and cheerful tricks that have saved me on multiple occassions!

1. Are your thighs rubbing against each other in that miniskirt you're wearing on a hot summer day? Fear not. Take some baby powder with you in your bag. Apply the powder to your inner thighs to avoid red and itchy skin. Shake it, baby, and repeat whenever necessary!

HACK #1

RUBBING THIGHS THAT LEAVE YOU WITH ITCHY SKIN?

GIVE YOUR THIGHS A GOOD RUB WITH BABY POWDER

TADA!

2. Forgot your mascara? Oh no! Put a teaspoon in some hot water and (very carefully) rub the rounded side against your eyelashes, in an upward motion. The heat will temporarily lift your lashes to give your eyes a more open look!

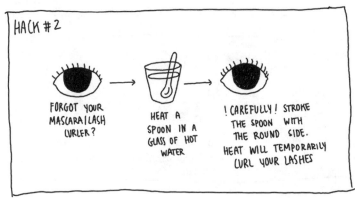

HACK #2

FORGOT YOUR MASCARA | LASH CURLER?

HEAT A SPOON IN A GLASS OF HOT WATER

! CAREFULLY ! STROKE THE SPOON WITH THE ROUND SIDE. HEAT WILL TEMPORARILY CURL YOUR LASHES

3. Make your own skin mask with stuff you find around the house!

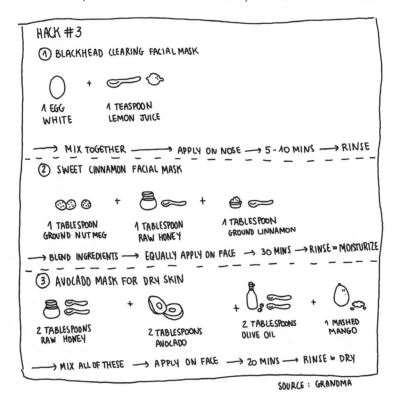

HACK #3

① BLACKHEAD CLEARING FACIAL MASK

1 EGG WHITE + 1 TEASPOON LEMON JUICE

→ MIX TOGETHER → APPLY ON NOSE → 5-10 MINS → RINSE

② SWEET CINNAMON FACIAL MASK

1 TABLESPOON GROUND NUTMEG + 1 TABLESPOON RAW HONEY + 1 TABLESPOON GROUND CINNAMON

→ BLEND INGREDIENTS → EQUALLY APPLY ON FACE → 30 MINS → RINSE ➣ MOISTURIZE

③ AVOCADO MASK FOR DRY SKIN

2 TABLESPOONS RAW HONEY + 2 TABLESPOONS AVOCADO + 2 TABLESPOONS OLIVE OIL + 1 MASHED MANGO

→ MIX ALL OF THESE → APPLY ON FACE → 20 MINS → RINSE ↳ DRY

SOURCE : GRANDMA

4. No eyeliner? No problem! Take a fine brush, dip it in some dark eyebrow or eye-shadow powder, and draw away! It will take a bit more time and precision work, but the effect is actually cool.

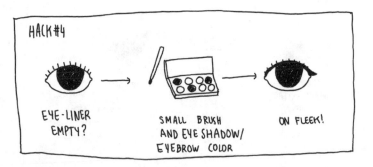

HACK #4

EYE-LINER EMPTY? → SMALL BRUSH AND EYE SHADOW/ EYEBROW COLOR → ON FLEEK!

5. If you can't afford those fancy candy-colored ChapSticks with fruity flavors, buy a jar of Vaseline instead. It's super cheap, fragrance-free and unflavored, and it's great stuff for multiple purposes: you can use it to treat chapped or dry lips, use it as an SFX makeup base, use it to hydrate dry skin that is very sensitive, or use it as eyebrow gel.

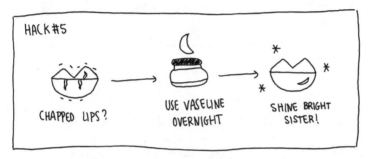

HACK #5

CHAPPED LIPS? → USE VASELINE OVERNIGHT → SHINE BRIGHT SISTER!

Bonus tip: I always put a dab of Vaseline on my lips before I go to sleep, so I wake up every morning with soft lips that can handle the heat or the cold.

6. Coconut oil is a great product for keeping your hair healthy and soft. Just put a couple drops on the dry or split ends of your hair after you shower. Result? Glossier and healthier ends! It also makes your hair easier to brush.

HACK #6

HAIR WITH DRY, SPLIT ENDS? → COCONUT OIL IS YOUR BEST FRIEND → EASIER TO HANDLE, GLOSSIER HAIR!

7. Here's how to turn every glossy lipstick into a matte one:

a. Put on your glossy lipstick as you normally do.

b. Take a tissue and pull it apart until you have one layer left. Press it against your lips.

c. Take a brush with some mattifying powder (or baby powder) and press it on the tissue.

d. Slowly pull the tissue from your lips and ta-dah! Soft and matte lips!

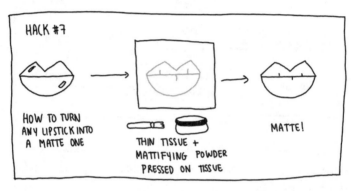

HACK #7

HOW TO TURN
ANY LIPSTICK INTO
A MATTE ONE

THIN TISSUE +
MATTIFYING POWDER
PRESSED ON TISSUE

MATTE!

8. Ran out of blush? Chrostin to the rescue! Take a red lipstick tube (or any color you like). Apply a tiny amount on your cheekbones and rub it in. Dab it with a beauty blender or brush and there you go: cheeky cheeks!

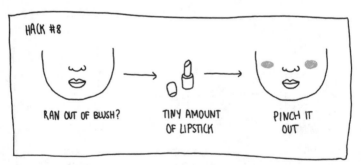

HACK #8

RAN OUT OF BLUSH?

TINY AMOUNT
OF LIPSTICK

PINCH IT
OUT

9. My lips can get a bit dry or chapped sometimes. A good scrub can make your lips feel soft and full again. Just take a pinch of kitchen salt and softly scrub it on your lips. Don't lick your lips, and

don't scrub too hard. Rub the salt in small, gentle circular motions for about thirty seconds. Rinse, dry, and feel the softness. Scrubbing your lips is great for removing dead skin cells and dry skin and makes it easier to apply lipstick after!

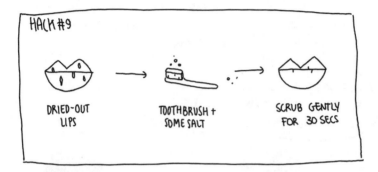

HACK #9

DRIED-OUT LIPS

TOOTHBRUSH + SOME SALT

SCRUB GENTLY FOR 30 SECS

Five Budget Tips for Going Shopping

Let's be honest, we've all been there: you literally *just* got your paycheck or babysitting money and *boom*—it's all gone. You couldn't help yourself. You simply *had* to buy that new thing, whatever it was—clothes, accessories, junk food, or snacks. Then the guilt usually kicks in immediately after you blow your freshly earned money. You start to think, *What have I done?*

If you want to avoid this kind of surprise in the future, here are some money-saving hacks that have helped me control my shopping addiction!

1. Run the numbers. Keep your receipts and calculate how much money you've spent in the past month. That's how you can keep track of the money that's going out the door. We tend to forget how much we've been spending, and that's why we sometimes have to gasp for air when we check our account balance. Assign categories to your purchases and expenses, so you can easily see what you spend the bulk of your money on. This also makes it easier to come up with a targeted plan to save some money here and there.

2. Ask yourself the following questions:
- How many of the things on this pie chart did I actually need?
- Can't I bring snacks from home instead of buying them on the go?
- Do I even have enough space for all the stuff I've bought?
- What made me buy this item? Am I actually using it, or did I just think it was cool/pretty/nice to have?

3. Imagine you are in need of new pants and you go out to buy a pair. A great way of going about this is to look for pants online so you'll have an idea of how much money you'll spend on the pair you want. Since they're pants, it's nice to be able to try them on before you decide to buy them, so I suggest going to a store to see how they fit you. Before heading to the store or mall, set your budget and take only *that* amount of money along. Don't bring extra cash or a credit card! Just bring along the amount in your budget. It might feel weird at first, but you'll feel grateful and proud of yourself afterward. Compare the price you found online to the price in the store and go for the best deal!

4. Keep track of the money you've saved. You can put that money in a piggy bank or jar or a bank account, and save it for

something special or important that actually costs a lot. Write the number on a sticker and put it on the jar, so you have always your goal in sight. Some top saving goals:

- a tattoo
- a trip (around the world or just down the road a bit)
- an expensive designer piece
- a new bike/car
- a new laptop/iPad/drawing tablet/etc.

5. Try thrift shopping. You'll be surprised how many gems you can find at thrift stores. Remember: Not all secondhand clothes are smelly or old-fashioned. I've scored a number of (otherwise expensive) designer pieces at secondhand stores or thrift shops for a very good price! There'll be more on thrift shopping later in this chapter.

6. Plan, plan, plan! Planning is everything. Did you save $5 this week? Great, write that down. That $5 will come in handy for the pair of shoes you want to buy so badly. Keep in mind that if you plan things beforehand, it becomes a *lot* easier to save money. It'll give you a sense of satisfaction when you manage to put money aside for something big you've wanted for a long time.

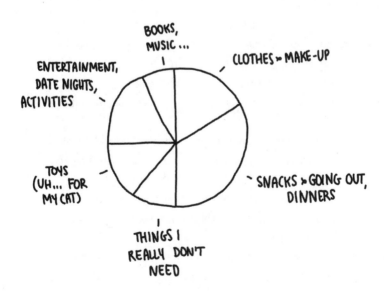

PEOPLE STARE AT ME WHEN I WEAR MY FAVORITE OUTFIT

Here's a scenario to consider. Every morning you wake up to the following choice:

1. You put on an outfit that you think is plain enough, so people won't stare at you. You play it safe so you'll blend in and won't be noticed. Or,

2. You wear whatever you like, because the only person that has to like your outfit is . . . you.

Wearing the clothes you like is a form of self-expression and a way of communicating how you feel, what you like, or what you stand for. You might even come across someone who has the same taste as you! People are social animals and value their culture of habits and social norms. There are several reasons why people might stare at you (there's a logical explanation for that, and it has nothing to do with you as a person):

• When your outfit doesn't match the dress code.
• When your outfit doesn't match the season. Wearing booty shorts and a tank top in winter will likely turn a few heads, but mostly because people are worried that you're freezing.
• When you're in a foreign country and local people are not used to your style.

So, what do you do when people stare at you and it makes you feel kinda weird? Try smiling! Flashing a smile is inviting and comforting to people, and 99.9 percent of the time that person will smile back. And even if they don't, they're probably so shocked that you smiled at them that they'll think twice before staring at someone again. Either way, you win.

It's okay for people to check out your outfit, as long as they don't judge or harass you for wearing it. You chose to rock your outfit today, so ... let them stare! You probably stare, too, sometimes, without even being aware of it. Mother Nature gave us eyes to stare at all the gorgeous outfits in the world!

Is it in people's nature to stare? Absolutely. But if you have social anxiety (see chapter 1 for more on that), you may be inclined to interpret people's stares as looks of disgust or disapproval, which they aren't (in most cases). This phenomenon is called *the spotlight effect*: you basically overestimate how much attention people pay to you or your behavior. To be honest, people don't care *that* much about you and are mostly preoccupied with themselves. So whenever you feel super self-conscious just remember the spotlight effect. Most people

aren't even aware that they're staring at you, because they are too consumed by their own thoughts.

BRAS

Why should you wear a bra? Well, you shouldn't, or at least not all the time. Scientists agree that wearing a bra *all the time* can cause health problems, while *never* wearing one can lead to a lack of support and possible back pain.

A bra is designed to support your boobs. It keeps them in place when you're playing sports, for example, and can help prevent breast tissue injury. If you have larger breasts, it's important to invest in high-quality bras that fit you properly in order to avoid back problems, muscle pain, and even headaches!

Finding out your bra size is really not that difficult. You can do it yourself or ask your mom or a sales rep to assist you. Don't be embarrassed to ask store assistants for help—they do this every day!

The following easy steps will help you determine your cup and bra size:

1. Take a measuring tape and put it around your rib cage right underneath your boobs. Pull tightly, but not too tight. Add 5 inches (12.5 centimeters) and round up to the nearest even number. This is your band size.
2. Now, measure the fullest part of your breast by putting the measuring tape around your boobs and across your nipples. Then, subtract the measurement from step one from the number you measured just now. The difference between these two is your cup size. 1 = A, 2 = B, 3 = C, 4 = D, 5 = DD, etc.
3. So, the first measurement (mine is 38) combined with your second measurement (mine is B, but sometimes C) = your bra size! Mine is 38B.

STRAPLESS

STICK ON

PADDED

BRALETTE

TRIANGLE BRA

CORSET

BANDEAU

T-SHIRT BRA

SPORTS BRA

UNDERWIRE

BALCONETTE BRA

PLUNGE

HOW TO FIND A BRA THAT'S BOTH CUTE AND COMFORTABLE

Honestly, a bra that is super gorgeous, super comfortable, and maybe even a little sexy at the same time is like a hidden treasure—it'll take you quite the journey to find it, and there are no maps to tell you where to look. Discovering a bra that suits your boobs and your (life) style perfectly might require a lot of fitting, searching, and groaning.

When my boobs started to grow (I was about fourteen years old), I simply went out to look for a bra that had to meet the following criteria: cute, cheap, *and* supportive. I soon found out that the best bras are usually not the cheapest. I had to lower my standards to match my budget and remove "supportive" from my list of requirements. And so I bought my very first A-cup bra: it was cute, it was cheap . . . but needless to say, the fit was a disaster. The band size I'd chosen was waaaaay too small and I ended up hurting my back and boobs.

It was not cute. At all. But even then, it didn't occur to me that maybe I was doing something wrong. I simply thought people wore bras like this all the time.

Remember that every brand and bra style fits differently. Don't hesitate to try out different styles, brands, or fabrics until you know what you like. Play around with the straps until your bra fits you at the shoulders. The bra shouldn't hurt your skin or make you feel strapped in, nor should it feel too loose around your breasts. Adjust the back strap until the bra feels secure but comfortable.

YOUR KICK-START TO THRIFT SHOPPING

One man's trash is another man's treasure. There are *so* many reasons why I love thrift stores: they're cheap, they sell unique stuff, and they are great for the community and the environment. The idea of finding something awesome for a very low price excites me to no end! Here's why we *all* should go thrift shopping more often:

1. The main idea of secondhand stores is that they are better for the environment than regular retailers that sell new clothes items, because most major brands nowadays produce clothing that isn't designed to last a long time. The quality of the fabric and stitching is often inferior to that of the clothes you find at thrift shops, too.

2. It's cheap. Like, super cheap.

3. You can actually find treasures at thrift stores. This is where I got my vintage Diesel jean jacket, some G-Star sneakers, cowboy boots, a fake fur coat, jewelry, several pairs of cool vintage sunglasses . . . literally everything I love to wear on a weekly basis.

4. It is always a surprise. You never know what you're going to find at a secondhand store. No monthly collections—everything is just super-limited edition!

5. If you have a pile of clothes you want to get rid of, the local thrift store is your best friend. Remember that the clothes have to be clean and ready for wearing when you bring them in for donation.

6. Did you know that thrift stores often hold huge discount sales? I'm talking sales on sales on sales!

7. Be careful about buying makeup at a secondhand store, though. While it's tempting to score highend makeup cheaply, make sure that the packaging is still sealed and check the expiration date, because expired makeup can cause irritation to your skin.

If this hasn't convinced you to at least check out a couple of thrift stores, I don't know what will. If it has, enjoy your first thrift store haul! But ahem . . . remember the budget hacks discussed earlier in this chapter and don't overdo it!

ACCESORIZING YOUR WARDROBE ON A BUDGET

Good news: you don't need expensive stuff in order to look awe-some. I used to make my own accessories from old pieces of jewelry, clothes, and thrifted goods. Chokers, necklaces, bracelets, and even earrings can all be found cheaply if you just take your time and find the right deals! It's so easy, and so much fun to do.

Psst! Handmade jewelry is also a cool gift idea! Here are some of my all-time favorite DIY-hacks for awesome jewelry and accessories:

1. The Choker
Why spend $10 on a necklace if you can make twenty of them for the same price? Here's what you'll need:

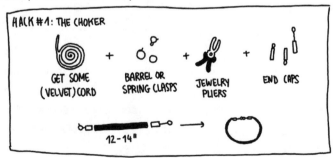

HACK #1: THE CHOKER

GET SOME (VELVET) CORD + BARREL OR SPRING CLASPS + JEWELRY PLIERS + END CAPS

12 - 14"

2. A Cool One-of-a-Kind Necklace

Not a fan of chokers? A necklace that no one else has can be just as cheap to make. You can find any type of plain necklace or chain in your local craft or hobby store. Next, look out for cool pendants, vintage or otherwise. You guessed it: thrift shops are the place to be for unique charms and pendants. You'll be the only one with a necklace this special!

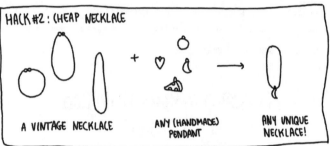

HACK #2: CHEAP NECKLACE

A VINTAGE NECKLACE   ANY (HANDMADE) PENDANT   ANY UNIQUE NECKLACE!

3. Pin It

Creating your own pin is super easy. First, choose the kind of safety pin you want to use. They come in various colors and sizes; I like mine gold-colored and small. Next, pick some beads, pearls, pom-poms, or whatever else you can pin through. This type of pin looks really cool on a denim jacket or a white shirt.

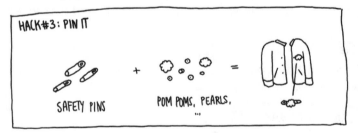

HACK #3: PIN IT

SAFETY PINS   POM POMS, PEARLS, ...

4. The Scarf

Who says your neck is only for wearing necklaces? You can find the cutest scarfs and shawls for just a few bucks. Whether you tie them around your neck or wrist, or put them in your hair, a pretty scarf is the perfect finishing touch to your outfit. Ta-dah! Multiple looks with just one accessory.

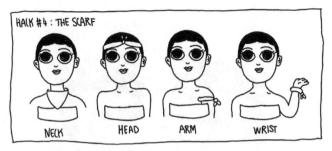

5. Second Life

Instead of throwing old items of clothing away, try giving them an update! Spice them up with awesome patches and buttons. It's cheaper than buying new clothes, but it looks like you've scored a new piece!

Don't throw away clothes that are eligible for reimagining! A bit of cutting, sewing, and stitching is all it takes to create a new wardrobe from items you have laying around.

Old jeans are really fun to get crafty with; they can be turned into shorts, scarfs, belts, or shoulder bags. So awesome. Are your pants a little boring? Choose a fabric in a color you like and cut two long strips. Stitch or sew them onto the side of your pants and voilà—a new, stylish, and fun look!

Chapter Five

FRIENDS AND FAMILY BUSINESS

Friends are the family you choose. But what about the family members you're stuck with? How do you survive that annual family gathering? How do you tell something difficult to someone you care about? Learn all about how to deal with friends and fam in the following pages.

THE DREADED FAMILY HOLIDAY GATHERINGS

Winter is coming (or maybe it's already here), and people are decorating their homes and front yards. The streets are beautifully lit and smell like warm family meals and happiness. Whether or not you celebrate Christmas, the hacks discussed in this chapter can be used to survive any awkward family celebration or holiday. I summed up some of the moments I frequently share with my family, but feel free to use your personal anecdotes as a backdrop to the topics brought up here.

A fun game to play with the younger members of the family is ...
Family Bingo! Just listen carefully to what others are saying and doing,
but don't make it too obvious. Create different versions for each
player (arrange the boxes in a different order on each of the charts)
and yell "BINGO!" if you can tick off three boxes in a row.

Here's an example, but feel free to insert catchphrases that are
typical of your family:

FAMILY CHRISTMAS BINGO

FUN GUARANTEED

EXCITING AND FUN TIMES!

"HOW'S SCHOOL?"	SOMEONE CAN'T STAND LOSING	"QUIT LOOKING AT YOUR PHONE AND JOIN US!"
SOMEONE WEARS AN UGLY X-MAS SWEATER	FAM MEMBER WANTS TO DANCE	SOMEONE YELLS ABOVE EVERYONE ELSE
FAMILY MEMBER STARTS TO CRY	SOMEONE MENTIONS A PAST INCIDENT	"IT'S DELICIOUS!"

1. The classic question: someone in the family asks if you have a boy- or girlfriend.

Don't be taken aback by the question, and don't let it make you feel
uncomfortable! Prepare yourself mentally. Answer calmly or jokingly,
both are fine. What you don't want to do is sit in silence, glaring
angrily, with a tomato-red face. The person who asked likely just
wants to know if someone is going to join the table at the next family
gathering. If you do have a special someone in your life, bring them to
the party. That way, they have to answer all the annoying questions
and you are safe for the rest of the evening. Yes!

You could also prepare some tricky questions yourself. Make them
awkward, like, "Auntie, where do babies come from?" or "Grandma,
do you believe in aliens?" Fun times and deep convos guaranteed.

2. You are constantly on your phone, avoiding awkward convos, and someone mentions it.

Maybe you only see your family once (or a couple times) a year. It's not going to kill you if you leave your social media accounts a little silent for just one afternoon or evening. You might miss some interesting discussions or developments at the family table if you are plugged into your phone all the time. Talk to your cousins. This is your family, and while you're there to spend time with them, you might as well get into it.

3. The grown-ups are getting drunk and starting to make racist comments.

Abort mission. I repeat: abort mission. Alcohol and family tensions are the perfect recipe for fights and traumatic holiday memories. Stay positive. Try to change the subject. Take one for the team and volunteer to share details about your personal life for once. Since everyone is so keen to hear about what's going on with you, this could put an end to their argument. If that doesn't work, walk away. Go play with the family pet or try to guess what's in the wrapped boxes under the tree. The kids shouldn't have to be the victim of grown-ups discussing stupid stuff. Make your own damn party!

4. You open a Christmas gift and are working really hard to hide your disappointment when the sender asks what you think.

You may remember this from chapter 1: telling a little white lie isn't always a bad thing. In this situation, you don't want to come across as a spoiled or ungrateful brat, and you certainly don't want to hurt your family member's feelings. They put time and effort into picking out a present for you. Give them a friendly nod, put on your poker face, force a smile, and say *thank you.* They will probably forget about this gift soon, anyway, and once you are out of their sight, you can always donate it to your local thrift store.

5. A family member accidentally blurts out one of your secrets. Everybody is staring at you right now.

Too bad, there's no coming back from this. There's no point in getting angry with the person as that will only lead to more tension. Damage control is the best policy; salvage the situation as well as you can. Calmly explain to your family what happened and give them some context to help them understand how you ended up doing what you did. Chances are your family will understand. After the festivities, have a proper discussion about what happened with anyone you feel needs additional explanation. You should also confront the person who spilled the beans; tell them they broke your trust and hurt your feelings.

Family gatherings are always unpredictable. Somehow, you know and also don't know what to expect. It's normal to feel anxious about this. Just try to enjoy your time together and everything will be cool. (And remember, it's only a small amount of time, so you can make it through!)

BREAKING DIFFICULT NEWS TO FRIENDS OR FAMILY

Having to tell something unpleasant or difficult to someone is never a fun thing. Your hands get sweaty, your heart rate increases, you feel stressed out—we've all been there once or twice, haven't we? But after telling your difficult news, you'll feel a thousand times lighter. Here are some methods that helped me get through a number of tough conversations with friends and family:

Situation #1: You have to tell your parent(s) about something you've done wrong. To illustrate this, I'll use the example of getting a very bad grade in a class. Failing in school is a stressful thing on its own, but having to show your bad report card or grades to your parents and seeing their disappointed looks just makes it twice as painful. So here's how you can go about breaking the bad news to them:

1. Prepare yourself for the conversation. First, calm down. If you're not calm, they won't be calm. Remember that getting a bad grade is something that happens to almost everybody at some point in their school career. Perspective is everything.

2. Choose honesty and tell them you screwed up or that you didn't understand the material and didn't ask for any help. It may be tempting to hide the truth, but believe me, it will come out in the end and you'll be in even bigger trouble if you choose to sit on it for a while.

3. Plan your conversation with your parents and do a small run through in your head. If possible, talk about it with your teacher first; maybe (s)he can help you by setting up a study plan to show to your parents. This shows that you acknowledge the gravity of the situation and are already taking steps to improve it.

4. Choose the right time and a comfortable location to tell them about your bad grades, such as your living room or your bedroom. Allow them to have some time first after they come home from work before you hit them with the news.

5. Sit down, take a deep breath, and calmly explain how it all happened. Perhaps you didn't study enough? Maybe you didn't understand the material fully? Or is there something else going on? Talk about it—now's the right moment.

6. Explain to your parents how you are going to address the problem. Maybe suggest getting a tutor or a study buddy? Let them throw in their two cents: if you allow them to contribute to the plan, they'll feel involved and helpful.

7. Most of the time, your parents will understand and support you no matter what. They might give you a fair punishment because you didn't study hard enough. Or they might insist on helping you prepare for the next test. Anger or frustration on their part are also normal reactions; they want to see you do well at school. However, if they attack you (verbally or physically), make sure to talk with someone about this, because that is not a normal reaction. That is abuse.

A bad grade is not the end of the world, and it can be fixed easily. But what if you have something far more serious to tell your parents? What if you're worried that your parents will kick you out of the house because of what you're about to say?

Situation #2: Your best friends know that you like girls. They are cool with it. You haven't told your parents yet, but you finally feel ready to do so. While coming out can be a great relief for many LGBTQIA+ teens, it's an incredibly difficult thing to do so it's important to prepare well for this talk with your family. To do so, follow these guidelines:

1. Write everything down in a bulleted list—what you think, how you feel, what you want to say. Getting really nervous and blacking out right before the talk is not uncommon, but it's very inconvenient. If you get tongue-tied, at least you'll have put your notes in writing and can use that to help you get across what you wanted to say.

2. Decide how you want to tell your family. Are you a good writer? Send a letter or an e-mail. This is a great option if you're afraid of their first reaction. A phone call is more intimate, and you always have the option of hanging up if you have to. If you feel confident enough, tell them in person. You can also do so in a very creative way, such as a short video or animation, or a drawing or painting. Or even a song, why the heck not?

3. Prepare yourself for the questions they'll ask. If you anticipate the things they'll want to know, you'll be better equipped to give them a confident answer.

4. All the while, you should remember that being gay or bi (or something else) is totally cool. No matter how your parents react, know that you are a valuable member of society and that you're not alone.

5. If your parents don't know much about the LGBTQIA+ community, inform them any way you can (assuming they're open to learning about it). You can point them to articles, helpful websites, films, documentaries . . . anything that can help them understand where you're coming from.

6. Give them some time. This kind of news can be a total shocker to parents. Don't worry, though: these things take time to process (unless they've known or suspected all along and aren't surprised at all).

7. If the conversation escalates to an argument and you feel unsafe, contact someone close to you who you can trust. Find a safe space where you can be yourself. Call a friend or the police if things get out of hand.

HOW TO STOP SIBLINGS FROM BORROWING STUFF WITHOUT PERMISSION

I have a younger brother, and a big part of our relationship consists of arguing about stuff we borrowed from each other without asking permission. If you notice that your sibling has taken something from your room for the millionth time without asking, and you want the thievery to end, here are some quick ways to help you settle the matter:

SIBLINGS

1. Talk about it. I can hear you thinking, *Don't you know that I've tried that already?* I'm sure you have, but I'm talking about a proper, grown-up conversation. Write down the reasons why you don't like it when people take stuff from your room. Don't yell or lose your temper with your sibling when you're discussing this. You won't get your point across unless you stay calm, and they won't learn anything. Also, losing your sh*t will make it harder to bring the topic up again, and in the meantime, they'll feel free to keep "borrowing" your things. If you're lucky, they might feel guilty and stop doing it for some time, but just know it probably won't be forever.

2. If a warning has no effect, you could try locking your room when you leave the house (if your parents will allow it, of course). Another option is to hide your stuff in random places or to take a picture of your belongings before you go out. That way, you can compare the picture to the state of your room when you return. One time, I even went as far as to spread cooking flour all over the floor so that I could tell by the footprints if someone had been trespassing in my room while I was away.

Completely paranoid, right?

The downside to this method is that it's very time consuming, plus you may lose your own stuff because you can't remember where you put it.

3. You've probably already tried methods 1 and 2 at some point, so I'd like to suggest a third way to solve this issue: open your closet and your other possessions to your siblings and invite them to borrow your things. Allow them to use whatever they want on two conditions: they have to promise to put everything back where they found it, and they have to agree to let you borrow anything you like from them as well. You can't wear all of your clothes or use all of your stuff at the same time, right? So why not let them borrow something if they really want to? If they break your agreement, though, you can involve your parents. Also, take a look at what it is that your siblings always borrow. Is it the same item over and over again? Perhaps it's a sweet idea to give it to them if they love it so much, and treat yourself by replacing it with something you'd really like to have instead.

If none of those methods work, getting angry is still not a good option. Try to explain why you are so upset with your sibling when they borrow things without your permission. If they learn to understand the impact of their behavior, they'll be more likely to change it (or at least one would hope).

REAL FRIENDS VS. FAKE FRIENDS

If you want a quick friendship test, use the checklist on the next page to evaluate your friend's behavior. But remember: this checklist can only give you an indication of whether your friend is real or fake.

BREAKING UP IS HARD TO DO . . . ESPECIALLY AMONG FRIENDS

Sometimes we have to break up with people in our lives. And some of those people, unfortunately, are our friends. Friendships can end because you slowly drifted apart or because one of you had to move across the country. Or maybe you stopped being friends after a huge, terrible fight. Whatever happened, in a lot of cases it's okay to just let the friendship go. If it was meant to be, you'd still be friends, or you may even be friends again in the future.

A REAL FRIEND

- ☐ ASKS HOW YOU'RE DOING AND LISTENS TO WHAT YOU'RE SAYING
- ☐ KEEPS YOUR SECRETS SAFE
- ☐ GIVES SINCERE COMPLIMENTS
- ☐ KNOWS YOUR QUIRKS
- ☐ MAKES OR BUYS YOU A GIFT
- ☐ OFFERS YOU A SHOULDER TO CRY ON
- ☐ WANTS YOU TO FEEL COMFORTABLE
- ☐ VALUES YOUR OPINION
- ☐ NEVER AWKWARD SILENCES
- ☐ TEXTS YOU RANDOMLY
- ☐ CAN KEEP A PROMISE
- ☐ MAKES YOU FEEL CONFIDENT
- ☐ OFFERS TO HANG OUT
- ☐ IS ALWAYS THE SAME
- ☐ ACCEPTS YOUR DIFFERENCES
- ☐ FORGIVES YOU
- ☐ RESPECTS YOU, EVEN WHEN YOU DON'T AGREE
- ☐ FOLLOWS UP ABOUT THE CURRENT EVENTS IN YOUR LIFE
- ☐ IS ACCOUNTABLE
- ☐ MAKES YOU FEEL GOOD FOR NO REASON
- ☐ WOULD TRY TO BE FRIENDS WITH YOUR PARTNER
- ☐ TRIES TO DEFEND YOU

- ☐ ...
- ☐ ...

→ ADD YOURS!

A FAKE FRIEND

- ☐ DOESN'T REALLY SEEM TO CARE ABOUT HOW YOU FEEL AND CHANGES THE SUBJECT QUICKLY
- ☐ TELLS YOUR SECRETS TO OTHERS
- ☐ SECRETLY DOESN'T THINK YOU CAN HAVE NICE THINGS
- ☐ IS NOT INTERESTED IN KNOWING YOU
- ☐ FORGETS YOUR BIRTHDAY EVERY YEAR
- ☐ DOESN'T REALLY HELP WHEN YOU'RE SAD OR UPSET
- ☐ OFTEN EMBARRASSES YOU (IN PUBLIC)
- ☐ WANTS TO BE THE BOSS
- ☐ AWKWARD SILENCES
- ☐ ONLY TEXTS YOU WHEN THEY NEED SOMETHING FROM YOU
- ☐ OFTEN BREAKS A PROMISE
- ☐ IS PASSIVE-AGGRESIVE
- ☐ HARDLY EVER/NEVER INVITES YOU
- ☐ ACTS DIFFERENTLY WHEN IN GROUP
- ☐ MOCKS YOUR INTERESTS, STYLE, TASTE...
- ☐ POINTS OUT EVERY LITTLE MISTAKE YOU MAKE
- ☐ VALUES THEIR OPINION OVER YOURS
- ☐ NEVER ASKS ABOUT THE STUFF HAPPENING IN YOUR LIFE
- ☐ NEVER SEEMS TO BE AVAILABLE FOR YOU
- ☐ MAKES YOU FEEL GUILTY FOR NO REASON
- ☐ IS JEALOUS OR TRIES TO HIT ON THEM
- ☐ GOSSIPS ABOUT YOU

- ☐ ...
- ☐ ...

It's okay if you feel like you and your friend are not the same as you were in the beginning of your friendship. People change, all the time. You are changing even as you read this. Maybe you've had a series of arguments with your friend or you simply don't enjoy your time together anymore. Perhaps you've figured out that your friend is actually a fake friend (run the checklist on page 103 to find out). There are various reasons why friends suddenly stop liking each other, and that's perfectly normal. There are quite a few ways to cut off a friend, and while none of them are pleasant, the relief once it's over can be satisfying. You can literally feel the weight being lifted off your shoulders, and you'll be able to start enjoying other things in life again.

Deleting your former friend on all social media and blocking her number without further explanation might seem like the easiest way to end a friendship, and she'd definitely get the hint, but it might not be the best way to go. She'll likely feel offended or upset, and you'll probably have to face her again one day, anyway. Save yourself the awkwardness of having to explain why you blocked her and handle the situation proactively, like the mature person you are.

Instead of cutting your friend out of your life, you can consider giving your friendship another chance and voice your concerns about your changing relationship first. Maybe the other person wasn't even aware that you've been feeling this way, and maybe she's willing to change the thing that bugs you about her. In that case, you can choose to try to make this work again. If the other person agrees to part ways, you can both close this chapter in life like two adults. No fighting, no hard feelings, no anger. Just life. This break-up scenario saves both of you a lot of hurt, and you also get the chance to ask any remaining questions you might have about why the friendship is ending. The same goes for your soon-to-be-ex-friend.

Just remember that breaking up with someone is not always easy (and it sure as hell isn't fun), but it's often the healthiest choice in the long run. You have the power to decide who you want in your life and who you want to let go. Be sure to prepare yourself before you walk into the conversation, so you're ready to deal with the aftermath.

Remember to stick to your guns and guard your boundaries. If you have to, cut off all communication with that ex-friend, including social media.

The most important message I can offer you is to take care of yourself. The breakup is going to sting a bit in the beginning, but the pain will fade away. If your ex-friend becomes emotional and refuses to accept your decision at first, that's normal. Give her the time she needs to process and accept this new stage, especially if she didn't really see this coming.

IT'S NOT YOUR FAULT: HOW TO DEAL WITH PUSHY FRIENDS

"C'mon. Just one drink. You'll feel so much more laid-back," friends tell me at a party. And even if I don't feel like drinking, I agree to it anyway, so that my friends won't make fun of me or so I won't feel left out. What you experience in this kind of situation is called *peer pressure*, and it happens when people encourage you to do things that you, deep down, don't want to do. But you're facing a very difficult battle. Do you stay true to yourself, or do you follow the rest of the group in their decision, even if you don't feel comfortable doing so?

It's not just kids or teenagers who have to deal with pressure from their peers: adults face this, too, and more often than you'd think. People give in to peer pressure because we want to fit in and be appreciated, or because we fear that we'll be made fun of if we don't play along. Peer pressure is not always a bad thing, which makes it difficult to tell when it's okay and when it's not. An example of positive peer pressure can be when your friends or family members encourage you to try something new or to enrich yourself and grow as a person.

Alison Bell, who writes for *Teen* magazine, has listed some great tips to avoid (negative) peer pressure. With the help of her tricks, I made this list, and I swear by it:

1. Say no like you mean it. Body language says it all, honestly. If you sound hesitant and stare at the ground when you try to say no to something, your friends/peers will pick up on that and push you even more until you give in.
2. Remember that you don't need to have a reason to say no. No means no, always. When your friends ask why not, just say, "Because I don't want to."
3. Don't buy into the bullsh*t that "everybody's doing it." Not everybody's doing it, I promise.
4. Don't pressure others!
5. Evaluate your friendships. True friends don't constantly push you to do stuff you aren't comfortable with or don't want to do. Learn how to get rid of fake friendships earlier in this chapter.
6. Remove yourself from the situation and from those friends! Leave. Exit. You don't have to stay somewhere you don't feel comfortable.

When you're entering college (or even in some high schools), peer pressure can get even trickier to navigate. Pressure might be put on you to use drugs or alcohol, to have sex, or to do something to someone else, like bullying. Some students cave in to the pressure because they have low self-esteem or because they're having a hard time figuring out who they really are.

We constantly look for approval from our peers, because their apporval means we are accepted and part of the group. But if peer pressure is the glue that holds the group together, this sense of acceptance is actually fake, and it might leave you feeling empty instead of fulfilled.

If your friends are pushing you to drink, to do drugs, or to go out when you don't feel like doing those things, they might say that you are "boring" or "weak." Alcohol, drugs, and parties might be their main source of entertainment, and they might believe that this is what college is all about. But don't fall for it; you don't have to feel the same way or act like they do.

Yes, we all want to have fun, but having fun can mean something totally different to you. And that's cool, too. If your friends don't respect that, it might be time to find other friends who share the same values and interests as you.

I love a great party every now and then. I can dance all night long and not touch a single drop of alcohol. Not because I'm against drinking on principle, but I just don't need it to have a blast. Also, I remember everything the next morning and I get to wake up feeling abso-lutely fresh. No hangover for me. Do my friends judge me for that? No, because they are awesome and respect my choices, my body, and my decisions.

let's do a bunch of illegal stuff and get in deep trouble !!

Or let's make some-thing of our lives and help the environment re-cover from our pollution !!!

Conclusion? Saying no doesn't make you a loser or weak. Actually, it means you have enough self-respect to make the choices you're comfortable with. And that, my friend, is what people look up to! You're hella strong when you stick to your guns and do what you want.

DIVORCES SUCK, BUT HERE'S HOW TO SURVIVE THEM

Divorces suck. My parents got divorced when I was nine years old, so I don't remember all that much about what it was like before when we were still a "happy family." My dad used to work night shifts, and my mom went away a lot during the day for work. I don't blame them for splitting up. When a relationship doesn't work, there's no point in forcing two people to love each other. Maybe if they'd stayed together for the kids (my brother and me), growing up would've been a bit easier for us. But I honestly wouldn't know, because they decided to part ways.

It didn't take very long for me to understand what was going on between my parents, but I bet it was very hard for them to tell us about their decision to split up. Having my parents decide to get a divorce was one thing, but when they told us they both had new partners already, that hit me like a truck. So right away, my parents basically quashed my hopes of them getting back together one day. I hated the idea of other people invading our little family. I even hid my mom's new wedding ring once, because I didn't want her to be with a guy who wasn't my dad.

I have to admit that I wasn't always the easiest child to cope with, especially when I was a young adult. I was a teenager when I met my stepparents, so things weren't always that easy. I was a teen, and an angry one at that. Nothing was fair, according to me. So I had a very hard time accepting my stepparents. I didn't have a stable relationship with either of them. Eventually, I think these experiences made me the confident person I am today. Stepparent-stepchild relationships aren't always bad, though. Some kids get along fine with their stepparents, or even become closer to their stepparents than to their actual parents.

Maybe your parents are going through a divorce right now, or maybe they're recently separated. Parents get divorced for various reasons. Maybe their relationship just wasn't working anymore, or maybe there was a lack of communication, alcohol or other drug abuse, domestic violence, money issues, general unhappiness, cheating . . . the reasons go on and on. It's very normal to be riding an emotional roller coaster during the divorce process and even for a long time after the divorce becomes final. You have to adjust to so many changes in your everyday life, and that's a lot to take in all at once. You can experience stress, loneliness, anger, anxiety, guilt, or sadness. But maybe you'll also feel relief and happiness that some changes have been made to put an end to a very stressful situation at home.

Whatever the reason for the divorce, you're going to have to deal with the outcome either way. Some changes will affect your daily life, so you might as well be prepared for them. Custody arrangements may be implemented and you/the court will have to decide which parent you are going to see when and for how long. Which parent are you going to live with? Then there is the question of moving: Do you have to move all of your stuff or just part of it? And what about school? Do you have to change schools? How will your other family members react to the divorce? Are you still talking to them? Can you count on them when you feel upset?

The process is going be a rough one, but you should always remember that none of it is your fault. You didn't choose to be in this situation, right? It's important that you reassure your parents that you love them both equally (if you want to stay in touch with both of them, that is). Your parents should never try to put you in the middle or use you as a person to complain to about the other parent. If they do, tell them their behavior upsets you and that you don't want to pick sides.

Take as much time as you need to get over the pain and stress the divorce has caused you. Some people are okay with it after a few weeks; others take years to accept it. Even many years after the divorce, it's okay if you still have very strong feelings about it.

And it's not unlikely that you will still have strong feelings about it after a couple of years, because that's when you might have to wrap your head around even more changes. Maybe you are now in a new family situation. Your parents might find a new partner, and maybe you'll have stepbrothers and stepsisters. Or what about a new baby entering the picture? Or what if one of your parents has a same-sex partner? It's normal to have completely new feelings about this. It's all right to vent these emotions to both of your parents. Many teens make the mistake of keeping their feelings to themselves. It might be good for you to write them down, draw them out, or talk about them. Going for a walk or playing sports can help to release tension caused by changing family situations, too.

HOW A DIVORCE CAN FEEL

Last but not least, look for a person who you trust and can talk to. It could be a friend or a family member (like your grandparents, brothers or sisters, uncle or aunt . . .) but sometimes it's a good idea to talk to a health-care professional as well. They can give you advice on how to deal with your specific situation in the way that's best for you.

CREATE YOUR OWN PRIVATE SPACE

Privacy can be hard to get sometimes, especially when you have to share a room with one or more siblings. Even if you have your own room, family members might still burst into your room without warning. Trust me, I've been there. I had to share an attic room with

Chapter Five: Friends and Family Business

my younger brother for many years, which became super weird when I started turning into a woman. Undressing became uncomfortable; I couldn't chat with my girlfriends privately on my computer or on the phone; even listening to music or watching TV became tough, because we had completely different tastes. But what if you do have your own room, but still feel like you have no privacy?

You can start by talking about it. Most of the time, your family isn't even aware that they're being annoying. Start by telling them what you're doing or planning on doing in your room. Say that you're playing an online game or working on a school project. Or tell them when you're having someone over and you want to spend some alone time without interruption. Build enough trust so your parents don't have to come into your room for an unimportant reason. If you prove that you're responsible and trustworthy, your parents will stop treating you like a little kid.

Of course, trust comes with a price tag. If you want to be treated like an adult, you have to behave like one. Remember that your parents are still responsible for you and don't want you to get up to weird stuff. And yes, they have the right to at least ask what you're doing.

Other quick tips to gain more privacy or trust in your house are:
- Put a password on your devices. And make it one that's hard to crack.
- Incognito function on your web browser is your best friend.
- Don't leave stuff in your room that actually belongs somewhere else in the house, like plates and glasses. That way, no one has a reason to go into your room to collect them.
- Reassure your family that you're doing well. Or if you're not doing well, tell them so. The more you involve your family in your life, the more the trust will grow.
- Help your parents around the house. If you're active in the household, your family will be grateful and treat you like an adult more.

Privacy is a matter of trust, mutual respect, and decency. If you show that to others, they'll show it to you, too.

Copy this door hanger, cut it out, and hang it on your doorknob.

Chapter Six

LOVE IS BEAUTIFUL/SUCKS

Why does love feel like you're flying but can also feel like you've been hit by a truck? Love is a very difficult topic to understand but ... maybe we don't need to understand it at all.

ON BEING IN LOVE AND WHAT IT DOES TO YOU

There is no clear definition that describes what it feels like to be in love, because the feeling can be different from person to person. The super strong feeling that you might experience in the beginning of a relationship is called *infatuation*, and it can turn into real love later on.

Is there a specific sign that tells you when you are in love? No. But your own gut feeling can tell you that you are. You might feel a warm and fuzzy sensation when you think about that specific person. The thought of them makes you happy and puts a smile on your face for no reason.

When I fell in love for the first time, which was in 2011, it made me stop thinking rationally for a while. Everything I did (or didn't do) was controlled by my intense emotions. I couldn't eat, sleep, or study for weeks, because it felt like I had a million little worms in my stomach. I was constantly thinking about my crush, and it made me so incredibly happy. It took a lot of courage for me to finally ask him out . . . and we recently celebrated our five-and-a-half-year anniversary together. How did I know it would work out? I didn't.

We went to the same high school, so I saw him every day. I carefully picked out my outfits and tried to look extra cute when I knew there was a chance I could *randomly* bump into him. Maybe it's a bit creepy, but I kinda remembered when and where he had classes, so I took the longer route to my own, just so that I could see him for a few seconds. The things you do for love, right? I remember making so many drawings and love notes for him (he now has three shoeboxes filled with my creations).

I was only fifteen at the time, but I just knew that I was in love. People often told me that it was puppy love, but I just felt like he was the right guy for me. Love is a feeling, honestly. So, when do you know you're in love? To me, it was when I caught myself doing stupid things to get his attention. I didn't pretend to be dumber or cooler than I was (that's just not how I roll), but I just made an extra effort to get him to notice me. A few months later, the happy buzz

of excitement slowly wore off and made room for real, genuine love. I felt the desire to take care of our relationship, to work hard so we could have nice things and travel together.

Being in love feels a bit like a warm blanket on a winter evening. Or an ice-cold drink on a blistering-hot summer day. Or like taking a sweet chocolate bath. For a while, being in love can make you feel like you have zero problems or stress. Being in love can make you feel like you're surrounded by ten of the cutest puppies you've ever seen. Or kittens, if you're a cat person.

It also makes you feel good about yourself, because if your love is reciprocated, it means the other person sees something in you that's worth loving. You open up to the person you are enamored with, which is a risk you take because it makes you very vulnerable, but your intuition tells you that it might be worth it.

We can't help falling in love: our brain makes a strong cocktail of chemicals and substances that make us feel this way. Some scientists even say that being in love is similar to having an addiction—and, well, they're not wrong. You become addicted to your lover's presence, their words, their attention. Sometimes, a part of our brain can suddenly wonder why we fell for this specific person, because "they're not even that attractive" or "they're kinda weird," but maybe that's exactly why you like them. When you're in love, like really in love, the feeling goes way deeper than just physical appearance: you like the other person because you find them funny, witty, smart, geeky, cute, sweet, etc. Your feelings might scare you a little bit in the beginning, but that fear will slowly fade away as you give in to the beautiful feeling of being in love, and you won't care about what other people think about you two, either.

Are you still not sure if you're in love? Here are a few telltale signs of being struck by Cupid's arrow:

• You light up when you hear or see the other person. Your heart might skip a beat when they text you. Their presence, not just their attention, gives you a sensational feeling and can make your whole day.

- You can't quite explain why you like them. It's . . . everything! The way they talk about their passions, their smile, their interests, the way they do things, and so on.
- You don't doubt it anymore: you are sure that you like this person. And you want them to like you back.
- When you're watching a romantic movie, you picture yourself and the person you like doing the things you see onscreen.
- You are always talking to them in your head, having nonstop imaginary conversations. Daydreams in which you invent all sorts of scenarios about the two of you are also very common.
- You never really want to say good-bye to them.
- You feel nervous and shy when you're around them.
- You're always either waiting for a text from them or thinking about the next thing to text to them.
- Everything they say seems super interesting, even if it's not.
- You start to feel responsible for their happiness and you want to make them happy, too.

Wherever you two are, you feel complete, like you don't need anything else to be happy at that moment. Everything feels right. You love each other despite (or maybe for?) your quirky sides. You can stop pretending to be someone else and finally be who you truly are, which feels . . . like coming home.

UNREQUITED AND UNRECIPROCATED LOVE

One-sided love sucks. It sucks bad. If you've ever liked someone but your feelings were unrequited, you know what it's like when you can't be with the person you want and feel undesired at the same time. It's weird, because your heart is broken before you even have a chance at a relationship. It can be a devastating feeling. And it can hurt your ego, too. But there are some things you can do to help deal with unanswered, unattainable love.

You can't help who you fall in love with; it's not a rational decision. It's all about emotions, and those are hard to control. So, first of all, don't blame yourself for loving someone. If that person doesn't reciprocate your love, just know that it's not you, but the situation. Maybe there's a logical reason why that person rejected you. Maybe the

other person has a significant other you don't know about or a different sexual orientation. Maybe that person is not ready for a relationship or are just not interested in being in one. Whatever the reason is, I have good news for you: you can get over it.

1. First of all, stop questioning yourself. We are quick to find all sorts of flaws and blame ourselves for not being loved back by our crushes. This can make you feel really insecure about yourself. You may start thinking, *What's wrong with me?* Hold on, sister, there's nothing wrong with you! We all look different and have different personalities, and it's okay if someone isn't attracted to you, physically or mentally.

2. Try not to take it personally. Again, it's not you; it's the situation you're both stuck in. Just imagine how difficult it must've been for the other person to break your heart. You can't choose who you fall for, and neither can other people. You know it's beyond that person's control, so why blame yourself for something neither of you can do anything about? You cannot push people to love you, right?

3. Don't be too harsh on yourself. For some reason, we tend to torture ourselves when we're hurt, but try to be kind to yourself. Don't punish yourself for something that's not your fault. Try to turn your disappointment into motivation and start taking care of yourself. Go shopping, get a makeover, take a trip, go for an adventure, talk more to people, go out more often, take a bath, learn how to cook, teach yourself to play the guitar, go work-out, have a girls night . . . you get the idea.

4. When we find out that our feelings for someone are unreciprocated, our natural reaction is to hit the pause button and wallow in our misery for a while. That's perfectly fine, but don't let this go on for too long. There's a time when you should try to unpause your life and start living again! Let's face it: you can't sit in your room waiting for that one person to love you back forever. There are literally so many people out there who'd be happy to meet you and, who knows, fall in love with you. But you're not going to bump into those amazing people if you hide away feeling sorry for yourself.

5. Take a step back. Maybe it's better for you to take some distance from the person who rejected you. It can help to unfollow them on all social media. You don't have to completely delete or block them, but make sure you do something so you're not constantly confronted with their face. Every time you see them after they've rejected you, it'll be like a little stab to the heart. And that will make it harder for you to move on.

Try to remember that heartbreak is something most people go through at some point, and the world is not going to end because someone doesn't love you back. There might come a time in your life when you reject someone. The more you allow yourself to learn from this experience, the quicker you'll be able to move on and meet someone awesome—someone who's worthy of your love and will love you back unconditionally. Being a teenager is hard; we all know that. We go through a lot of (growing) pains in our adolescent years. But they say time heals all wounds, and I'll tell you what . . . it really does.

HOW DO I ASK SOMEONE OUT ON A DATE?

According to a survey conducted by the Pew Research Center, the majority of American teenagers prefer being asked out on a date in person, despite the many social media options available today. Going the old-fashioned route and asking someone to go out face-to-face shows that you're willing to make an effort, take a gamble, and risk being rejected in person. I can definitely see how a digital rejection might be less hurtful and also be easier to forget.

First of all, it's perfectly okay for a girl to ask someone out. We live in the twenty-first century. Some people might even find it cool or ballsy; after all, it takes guts to confront someone in person. Whether it is for prom, homecoming, or just your average Saturday night, try to come up with a great way to ask your crush out.

If you don't know how your crush would prefer to be asked out, then maybe you don't know them well enough yet. Get to know each other a bit first, talk more often, become friends . . . you'll feel more confident when you eventually do ask them out. Instead of asking them out for an official date, you could ask them for a casual hangout to get to know each other some more. Whatever you do, don't expect a stranger to be your significant other after one date. Or two. I mean, it's possible, but it's not very likely. A guy once asked me out when I barely knew him. I felt awkward and uncomfortable and declined. If we had known each other a bit better, I might have said yes.

So, let's say you're friends with another person and you decide you want to ask him or her out on a date because your feelings for that person are more than just friends. Other than taking a blind guess and improvising a date at the last second, it's probably smart to give it some thought before the big day arrives. Where and how do you want the date to be? Do you want it to be just the two of you, or do you want to go somewhere other people can see you? Both have their advantages, but the important thing is that you feel comfortable with the setting you choose. Maybe meeting in public is not a bad idea for the first time.

Do you want to get cozy (like at the movies) or go for a night out dancing (like at a club)? Do you want to go out for coffee or are you more interested in taking a walk? If you know the other person a bit, you might already know what their interests and favorite activities are, so make sure you plan something they'd consider fun, too.

Okay, now that you've decided on where and what you want to do on the date, it's time to pop the question. How the hell do you do that? What if the other person says no? What if (s)he freaks out and doesn't want to be friends with you anymore? What if, what if, what if? Here's the thing: drop the "what if" attitude and go for it. You can't win if you don't play the game. And so what if the other person says no? You'll be hurt, but you'll survive.

Here are some practical ways to ask someone out:

• Try to do it in person. Most people appreciate it when you make an effort and put yourself out there. Also, you can see the other person's reaction immediately, which tells you a lot more about how excited they are (or aren't) than in a text or e-mail. I know it's scary; I've been there before.

• If you're better at writing down your feelings, then do that. Write him or her a letter, a love note, or an e-mail. Make it fun; love and dating are fun. Include a little coupon for your date-to-be. People appreciate a little humor or wittiness in a date invitation.

• This one might seem a bit creepy, but do some research. If you don't know each other very well, you can check their social media to find out more about what they like, what their interests are, or where they like to travel. You'll then have a wide range of topics to discuss and ask questions about. And let's be honest: you've already snooped around their accounts anyway, am I right?

• If you're too nervous to be alone with your crush, try a group date. Just a casual hangout with friends from your class or school. You'll have some time to talk with your crush in a comfortable environ-ment without the pressure of a one-on-one date. If you find yourself having awkward silence with your crush, then there's other people there to fill in the blanks.

Go for it! Take the jump and just ask if the person wants to go out with you. Worst-case scenario: you're turned down, but maybe that's not such a bad thing in the bigger scheme of things. If they reject you, at least you'll know how they really feel about you, and then you can move on. You can stop investing time in a relationship that wasn't going to work anyway. You deserve someone who's not only attracted to you, but who loves and wants you as much as you love and want them.

S-E-X:
LET'S TALK ABOUT IT

When are you ready to have sex? While some teens are "early birds" and others "late bloomers," don't be influenced by what others consider an okay age is to have sexual intercourse. Being ready to have sex is a decision or feeling that is 100-percent personal, so don't let anybody else call the shots on this one.

How old is old enough? It seems to be a never-ending and pretty pointless debate, because some teenagers are mature at a young age, while others seem to stay twelve forever. What I mean is: there isn't one benchmark age after which everybody is ready to have sex; it just doesn't work that way. From a legal perspective, both parties have to be at least sixteen years old (and in some states, seventeen or even eighteen). This is called the *age of consent*. You're allowed to have sex at or after that age according to the law.

So, that's where the problem starts: What if you feel ready before the legal age? Or what if you're old enough and you're not ready at all, but you feel pressured to have intercourse because your friends are doing it? And what if you and your significant other are under the legal age but feel ready?

The key to a healthy relationship with yourself and others is communication. Talk to someone about this huge moment in your life before you act on it. Maybe it's an older brother or sister, mom or dad, friends, a guidance counselor, your grandparents (why not?), or anyone else you trust. And talk to your partner, too. There's nothing wrong with wanting to talk about sex first, before actually having it. It's a pretty damn smart move, if you ask me. If you don't know how to get access to birth control, maybe your parents can provide it for you in the beginning. Free contraception is often available at community contraceptive clinics, sexual health clinics, some youth people's services, your doctor's office, and the like. Do a little research or ask friends to give you advice on getting contraceptives before you have sex.

BIRTH CONTROL TIPS

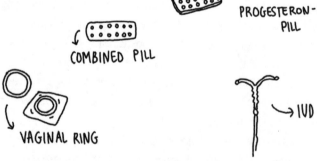

There is a wide range of options for contraception, including the following:

• male condoms: worn on the penis, available at pharmacies, supermarkets, vending machines in public restrooms, online, etc. They're very effective if used correctly. They stop a man's semen from coming into contact with his sexual partner.

Chapter Six: Love Is Beautiful/Sucks

- female condoms: worn inside the vagina to prevent semen getting into the womb; also highly effective if used correctly. You can find them in pharmacies, supermarkets, online, etc.
- progestogen-only pill: this "mini-pill" is an oral contraceptive pill, to be taken around the same time every day. This pill contains the hormone progesterone, but not estrogen. If taken correctly, it's almost 100-percent effective. It doesn't protect against STIs (sexually transmitted infections). Use the pill in combination with condoms to be completely safe. Some of them are available for free, but not all of them. Always talk to your doctor first if you want to start taking birth-control pills.
- combined pill: also known as "the pill," this is to be taken around the same time every day. This pill contains the hormones progesterone and estrogen. If taken correctly, it's almost 100-percent effective. It doesn't protect against STIs, though. Use the pill in combination with condoms to be completely safe. Apart from preventing pregnancies, it's also used for treating heavy or painful periods, as it helps release the tension and pain. Most types are available for free, but not all of them. Always talk to your doctor first if you want to start taking birth-control pills.
- vaginal ring: small, plastic ring that you put inside your vagina and remove after twenty-one days. This is also highly effective, and you don't have to think about it every day (like you do with birth-control pills), but it doesn't protect against STIs. Use in combination with condoms to be completely safe.
- an IUD: a little T-shaped device made from plastic and copper that's inserted into your uterus by a doctor. It's highly effective, and it can last up to five or even ten years, so you don't have to think about it every day. It doesn't protect against STIs. Use condoms too to be completely safe.

The overview I just gave is very brief, and it only covers some of the options out there, because those are the only contraceptive methods I have some kind of experience with. The most important thing about birth control is that you choose the method that fits you best. All of the options listed have their own advantages and disadvantages. I really can't stress this enough: talk to your doctor first so you can figure out which method is the most ideal for your body and lifestyle. Ask for more information or alternative options if you're interested.

Whatever you do, having unprotected sex should never be an option to consider. Even if you're in a steady relationship and you're both STI-free, you should think about the other consequences of having unprotected sex. It doesn't matter how healthy you are: you're always at risk of catching an STI or having an unwanted pregnancy. Even if you're sure you're clean, you might have an STI you're not aware of, because most of the symptoms are not noticeable. Just because you don't see or feel anything doesn't mean it isn't there! If you're really unlucky, you can catch an STD in a public toilet, by sharing a towel with your best friend, or by wiping in the wrong direction after going number two. Wearing the same underwear for too long or not changing your period protection frequently enough can cause problems, too.

In conclusion: if you and your partner both feel ready to have sex and to do it safely, there's only one important rule left to mention: have fun!

CHROSTIN'S FIVE ORIGINAL DATE IDEAS

Looking for an original date idea to do with your crush? Maybe you're in a relationship and you want to do something different for a change to spice up your romance? You came to right place, girl. Sit down, relax, and take a look at my five favorite dates.

*Spoiler alert: dinner and a movie are *not* on the list. Don't get me wrong—I love going to the movies or going out for dinner sometimes. But I mean, that's what we *always* do. I love surprises and I love surprising my date even more.

1. Build a Netflix-fort.
I used to do this with my s/o
when we were in the beginning
of our relationship. We thought
it was really cool to actually build
something together, and we had a
great hiding place to make out in
afterward while watching our
favorite Netflix shows. This is
a very cute date idea when
it's cold or raining outside,
but when you still want to

do something active. Also in the same category: have a pillow fight,
binge-watch horror movies in the fort, listen to some music, and just
chill or talk.

2. Be a tourist in your own town. You may think you know your
city, but you probably won't know everything until you see it through
the eyes of a tourist! Here's the trick: look for touristy attractions

in your town and plan a route.
Make sure to include breaks for
ice cream or coffee. Take lots of
pictures, like you've never been to
that place before. This date has
the added benefit of teaching you
more about your town.

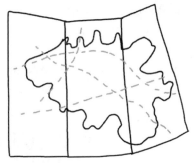

3. Take classes. Probably not
the best option if you and your
date aren't a real couple yet, because taking classes means you'll have
to attend them more than once. First, find something you're both
good at or at least interested in. It's an opportunity to learn new
things, *and* doing stuff together will make you and your lover grow
even closer. Win-win!

4. Host a game-and-snack night. Games can be either
digital or old-school boardgames, whichever you like. You both bring

snacks or drinks. Playing games together can teach you a lot about your date—maybe they're crazy competitive or super patient and helpful when you're struggling to get the hang of a favorite game. And people's true nature is always revealed if they lose! If you're not a gamer, but you do like a bit of adventure or competition, this could be your thing!

5. Cook together. Whether it's baking a cake, making dinner, or preparing lunch, cooking is a great activity to do together, *and* you have food afterward. It also gives you something to talk about, in case you're nervous or don't know each other that well yet. Either way, it's a good opportunity to share a meal together without spending too much money, too.

I absolutely love those five date ideas, but of course you can add more things to the list, depending on what you like to do. If you think outside of the tried-and-true date box, fun times are guaranteed!

ENDING A BAD RELATIONSHIP IN THE LEAST PAINFUL WAY

There are many reasons why you might be unhappy in your relationship. Does your partner call you names? Are they passive-aggressive, or even just plain aggressive? Do you feel alone and excluded, even when you're together? Are you in love with someone else? Is your partner extremely jealous or controlling? Does he or she make you feel bad about yourself, or force you to do things you don't want to do? Are you just generally unhappy or simply not in love anymore? Whatever the reason might be, it's probably best if you end your relationship sooner rather than later, because being together is likely unhealthy for you both.

REMINDER TO SELF: I WAS IN AN UNHEALTHY RELATIONSHIP AND PUTTING MYSELF FIRST IS NOT A CRIME!!!

REASONS WHY I BROKE UP (AND SHOULD REMEMBER WHEN THE PERSON TRIES TO COME BACK):

There is no "good" way to break up with your significant other. No matter what your reason for dumping them is, remember that open communication is key. Your partner might feel differently about your relationship and be shocked, sad, and hurt by the breakup. Try to talk your way through any conflicts that might arise. The good-bye-talk is a very difficult conversation to have and never fun to do or receive. You have to realize that you're going to hurt your partner's feelings no matter what you say, because rejection always hurts. But if you're honest and open, it can take the sting out of it a little bit for the other person.

There are a number of classic mistakes you might be tempted to make when you break up with someone. Sometimes people can't seem to be bothered to end things properly, but unless we do, the other person is left behind with a lot of questions and a lot of heart-break. And neither of you will have learned anything about having a respectful relationship.

Sometimes it's tempting to lie about the reason you're breaking up with your boyfriend or girlfriend. While this saves you the unpleasant task of hurting your partner's feelings, the truth will come out in the end and they'll be even more hurt because they didn't hear it from you first. So rip off the Band-Aid and spare yourself the future drama; honesty is the best policy here.

Another common mistake is breaking up via social media. If you two were in a committed relationship and shared some special moments together, you can't just end all of that with a WhatsApp message or Snapchat. Your partner deserves proper closure. Dumping someone online or via text will make that person feel like he or she never meant anything to you. I understand why it might seem easier to you, but it definitely doesn't help the other person.

Another strategy that is a no-go is to avoid having to dump your partner by getting them to dump you. It can be tempting to start being rude to your significant other, or to cheat, lie, call them names, or ignore them—anything to provoke them so they'll do your dirty work for you. Let me tell you: this kind of behavior will only make things worse, and it's not a fair way to end your relationship. Imagine if the roles were reversed; you wouldn't want people playing games with you like that, would you? The rule to live by here is to treat other people the way you'd like to be treated.

Take a look back on your relationship and try to figure out where things went wrong, in your opinion. Maybe there was a specific moment when something happened or changed. Maybe you can't pin-point it at all and have no clue why it didn't work out. It's normal for feelings to change. Having a change of heart is a legit reason to end a relationship, but you have to communicate that with your partner. Keeping your changed feelings to yourself will turn your relationship into a ticking time bomb that will explode sooner or later.

Once you've decided to have the tough talk, choose a comfortable and private location for you and your (soon-to-be-ex) partner—somewhere you are alone and no one can bother you. Make sure glasses of water are available, as is a box of tissues. Be up front and straightforward. Don't beat around the bush. Never blame the other person, but talk about yourself and your feelings instead. Be prepared for emotional outbursts and possibly a lot of questions, but hopefully at the end of the conversation, you'll have a clean break.

If the two of you agree to remain friends, that's amazing. If it's too painful for either one of you right away, though, it might take some time, or it might never happen where you can be just friends. This is a possible consequence you have to take into account before you break up with someone: you don't just lose your partner—you might also lose your friend.

Breaking up is never fun. Just approach the situation with care, because you're dealing with another person's heart here. If you handle the breakup with grace and empathy, it'll make it easier for the other person to get over you eventually. In the end, you'll both be able to put the past behind you and move on.

GLUING BROKEN PIECES BACK TOGETHER: HOW TO FIX A BROKEN HEART

A broken heart might be the worst feeling in the whole world. Maybe you're in love with someone who doesn't love you back, or maybe you've recently been dumped by your sweetheart. Perhaps you were cheated on, or maybe you recently broke up with someone yourself. That's right: just because a breakup was your idea doesn't mean it can't also hurt your heart.

It's normal to feel very sad for a while after losing someone you love, even if the other person has treated you with respect during the breakup. You might be in shock at first, especially if you didn't see the end of the relationship coming. There's no way of knowing for how long you'll be sad or upset. Some people only need a few days or weeks before they bounce back; others take months or even a year to completely recover from a breakup. It's important that you allow yourself some time to grieve. Cry as much as you have to, and for as long as you have to. After that, it's time to pick yourself up and start thinking about letting go.

Letting go is definitely easier said than done. Some people distract themselves by finding a rebound lover—someone they hook up with just to fill the void and get the affection they crave. That could work for a while, but be careful not to hurt that person's feelings after you are done rebounding. After all, you only started seeing them to get over your ex, but they may genuinely have fallen for you.

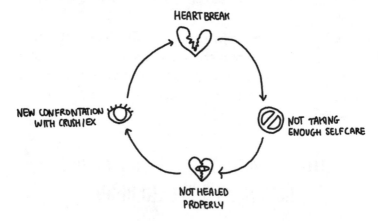

HEART BREAK

NEW CONFRONTATION WITH CRUSH / EX

NOT TAKING ENOUGH SELFCARE

NOT HEALED PROPERLY

As you gradually mend your broken heart, don't forget to take care of yourself and your body. Your physiological health is just as important as your mental health. Take your mind off your sad or negative feelings by getting some exercise, taking a long shower or a bath, going out for fresh air, writing down your thoughts, and so on. Talk to others about how you feel, and you'll see that there is so much more to life than mourning an ended relationship.

Staying in touch with your ex can be tricky as there are upsides and downsides to consider. Decide for yourself if you want to still be friends. It can be helpful to be able to talk to them about how you feel, even after you've broken up. Try to avoid making him or her feel guilty about dumping you (if that's the case), because that's not a nice thing to do and it won't get you anywhere. If you both are on friendly terms again and maybe even hanging out, this can stir up old feelings on both sides, so be careful about getting back together with your ex. Chances are that you both just miss the idea of having a relationship, rather than miss being a couple. If you decide that you don't want to keep in touch with your ex, that's okay, too. Just make it clear to your ex in a friendly and respectful way.

Whether you're the dumper or the dumpee, the end of a relationship always provides a valuable life lesson. What did you learn from this relationship? What can you do better next time? What were some other factors that led to the breakup? How big was your part in what went wrong?

Lastly, don't worry about finding a new significant other. Time really does heal all wounds, so you just have to wait and give yourself as long as you need. Once you're completely healed, you can start thinking about opening yourself up to a new love. In the meantime, allow yourself some recovery time and give yourself some credit for being as strong as you are. This is an opportunity for self-discovery and some self-love, too.

DEALING WITH AN EX: THE DOS AND DON'TS

Dealing with your ex can sometimes be a little tricky. You still might have a lot of feelings for this person, but deep down you know it's better for both of you to stay out of each other's life. Maybe you still have to face them because you go to the same school or have the same part-time job. And what if they start dating someone new—how will you cope with that?

It's important for you to heal first. You're hurt, upset, sad, angry, lonely, or jealous. And that's perfectly normal. You shared some of the happiest moments of your life with this person and all of the sudden they're gone.

It's normal to have very strong feelings about your ex when you see him again, or when you find out that she started dating someone new. Remember that your ex has the right to move on, too, even if that person does it before you. It's not a competition. Don't focus on being the first to get over your breakup but rather focus on your future and on healing your heart. Seeing your ex with someone new can be extremely painful, but learning that there's no more hope of the two of you getting back together might help you get over the relationship faster.

Here are some other tips to help you deal with your ex in a healthy way:

• **Try not to be overly jealous.** It's very normal to be jealous of your ex, especially when you see he is having a great time without you. Maybe it's his way of coping with the breakup. Don't worry too

STOP COMPARING YOURSELF TO YOUR EX'S NEW PARTNER. IT'LL DRIVE YOU CRAZY.

much about what your ex gets up to, and keep the reasons why you broke up in mind to help you get through the harder moments. Write down the reasons and read them over and over again. It makes it easier to get over your ex and to stop being jealous of everything he's (not) doing.

• **Stop comparing yourself to other people**, especially if your ex has a new partner. Like I said before: relationships aren't about who's the best, the prettiest, the funniest, or the smartest. If your ex had wanted to stay with you, that's what she would've done. Remember that it's the other person's loss, and that you don't have to compete with their new partner. You don't want to be the crazy, obsessive ex, right?

• **Don't stalk!** The less you see your ex, the less you have to think about him. Avoid the places you know he might be, unless you can handle a confrontation in a mature way. It might also be a good idea to avoid online stalking. It's obsessive and very destructive to your health. And it can be just as problematic as stalking someone in person. Be careful not to check out your ex on social media too often.

• **Talk about your feelings with others.** Have a chat with someone you trust and explain what you're feeling. A good friend will listen to you and offer you a shoulder to cry on when you need it. Just remember to vent your feelings from time to time; don't keep them all inside. Getting things off your chest will leave you feeling a little more relaxed and clearheaded.

• **Don't make your mutual friends pick sides.** The breakup is hard for you, but it can also be very awkward for your mutual friends. They like both of you, so it's unfair to make them choose between the two of you. Try not to gossip about your ex with them, either. You don't want to be *that* person.

Give yourself time, space, and freedom. Your daily life will be very different without your partner, but that doesn't necessarily mean that it'll be worse. Embrace your independence and focus on your personal goals while you have some time to yourself. You never know when that new and special someone will enter your life.

Chapter Seven

SCHOOL AND WORK, WORK, WORK, WORK, WORK

We spend the largest chunk of our days at school or at work. But what about the things we don't learn at school but still need in our (professional) lives? In this part you'll read more about how to survive high school, write the perfect résumé, be more productive, and so much more!

HIGH SCHOOL IS SO WEIRD!

To me, honestly, high school was the weirdest period in my life. I often look back on that time and wonder, "What was I thinking?" Between the ages of twelve and eighteen, I went through so many changes and transformations. I had so many different groups of friends, ended up at the weirdest parties and places, hooked up with the wrong people, and did many other strange things. I wore the craziest fashion, and in hindsight, I wonder why nobody tried to stop me from being so odd. I was constantly going back and forth between who I was and who I was trying to be. I had my heart broken, not just by people I had a crush on, but also, and worse, by people I considered my best friends.

High school was harsh; people were bullied, excluded, and picked on. People gossiped behind others' backs. High school was a game, really. It was one big competition to decide who was the prettiest, smartest, slimmest, coolest, or most popular. Nothing else *really* mattered. It was all about who said what about whom. Grades were only important if you were doing exceptionally well or disastrously bad. Everything and everyone in between was not interesting enough to talk about.

And they say high school is the greatest time of your life? Give me a break.

We all know high school can be a long, big chapter in our lives. We struggle with our identity, our grades, our love lives, our social statuses, our friendships, our time management, our health, our families, our daily water intake, and our mental health. I know I shouldn't complain; the education I received is a privilege and I'm grateful for the chances I've been given. I know I should feel

thankful to have been able to go to school at all, but that doesn't change the fact that high school is super weird! But why is it like that?

When we are teenagers, we are young, the world is ours, and yet we are expected to sit on a chair for eight hours each day, listening to someone explain something that we'll soon forget anyway. We try to concentrate, but we're thinking about hanging out with friends later. Or about what we might have for dinner that night. "Ring!" Finally the bell chimes for the day to end. We go home, and our parents ask how school went. We say, "Fine," like we do every day before escaping to our rooms. Before shutting the door, our parents ask, "What did you learn?" Nothing. Nothing at all.

You want to learn, but do you hate studying? Join my team. I was always excited to learn new stuff, about life and about the world. I found history very interesting and I always tried my best during gym class. But I wanted more. I wanted to learn how to cook, how to sew, how to do my taxes, how to survive a house fire, how to give CPR, how to wash my clothes, how to fix things that are broken, and how to properly paint a wall. My home situation was complicated, and I didn't get to learn all of those skills when I was a kid.

I can't even count the number of times I wondered how the stuff they taught me in school was in any way relevant to my own life. To me, high school seemed to be all about memorizing facts for the sole purpose of passing a test. Fun trivia, definitions, dates . . . that's why my grades were pretty average. It's not because I didn't care or didn't take an interest—I just wasn't very good at studying. I loved learning new skills and languages, but studying the names and functions of each cell in the human body just wasn't my thing.

Next: homework. I remember being incredibly anxious and stressed out *all the time* because of the piles of homework I had waiting for me after class. Time management wasn't my strong suit, and I was a real perfectionist, so I procrastinated on everything because I wanted it to be perfect before I handed it in. The result? I always finished my assignments at the very last minute, so most of the work was done in a rush since I didn't have any more time. Homework is a *huge* part of our stress in high school.

The homework issue brings me to another reason why high school is so weird: the expectations are absolutely insane. Some kids in my class got *so* nervous when they didn't get straight A's—not because they were disappointed by the grade or because they didn't put the work in, but because they were afraid that their parents or guardians would be angry with them. That's one thing that I could never wrap my head around: high school shouldn't teach kids to be afraid of failing. High school students are under so much pressure to achieve, but what good does it do them? It's a question I still haven't figured out, even four years after I graduated.

When I started college, I quickly learned that no one actually cared about other people's grades. Everyone was going through the same thing and that was what united us. There was no distinction between the people who got good grades and those who got bad grades.

It's true: it does get better after high school. People tend to say that college is very difficult, but in this sense, it's a lot easier. I wasted many years of my adolescence putting pressure on myself to live up to impossible standards. If I had the chance to do it all again, I'd spend more time on my personal development and growth instead of worrying about each little pop quiz.

Another reason why high school is so weird has to do with your age and puberty. Going to school can be difficult at any age, but it's ten times worse when you're a teenager. As a teen, you're expected to listen, behave, and succeed. And, big surprise, none of this works the other way around: grown-ups don't really listen to you because they insist that you don't know what you're doing, saying, or feeling. In the meantime, you're dealing with your first period, trying new things with your clothes and makeup, figuring out who your real friends are, and so on. You'll get boobs and hips and feel mostly confused about them. And oh, did that person just flirt with you? Not sure. That leaves you even more confused. You'll get hair in weird places, too, and wonder if you need to shave it or not. As if high school on its own isn't bad enough, going through puberty makes it even more unbearable.

Lastly, being popular (or not) can determine your entire high school experience. I used to have one main group of friends, but I was friendly with a lot of other people, too. I hated when people decided they couldn't stand others when they'd never even really met them. I wasn't the prettiest girl, but I had a great sense of humor that made me "popular" in a way. As I said earlier, high school is just a game, and it's not until you move on from it that you realize how ridiculous and meaningless the whole concept of popularity really is.

High school is weird for many reasons. It's mainly a combo of high expectations, puberty, age, the pressure to be popular, and the stress of homework. However awful it may seem right now, I can promise you it will get better. Soon, you'll be old enough to choose your own workplace, friends, and place to live. Does that scare you? I understand, because growing up *is* scary. For now, enjoy your time as a student. Both have their advantages!

HERE'S WHAT YOU CAN DO
IF SOMEONE IS BULLIED

Whether it's you or somebody else who's being bullied, it's always difficult to deal with this situation. Bullying is not always that visible at school (take cyberbullying, for example), which makes it even more difficult to tackle. If people were picking on you, you'd want someone to help you and stand up for you, right? So that's what you should try to do when you see someone else being bullied. But how do you intervene without seeming overprotective or making yourself a target for the bullies, too?

Letting that person know that you're there for them whenever they need you can already make all the difference in the world. Sit with the bullied person during lunch or breaks (not every day, not all the time, but occasionally) and talk to them. Don't give in to peer pressure, and don't let the bullies intimidate you. (Learn more about peer pressure and how to resist it in chapter 5.) It's important to remember that it's never okay to bully someone back. Don't fight fire with fire. It could even make things worse for your friend, and you don't want that on your conscience, right?

Before you do anything, you have to know for sure that the person you're trying to help is being bullied. It can be hard to get more information, because people who are bullied can be reluctant to talk about it—either because they are too upset or ashamed, or because they are afraid something will happen if they tell others what's been going on. The following are some red flags you can look out for: is the person absent from school a lot, or do they seem distracted in class? Have you heard any (nasty) rumors about them lately? Are they being left out during breaks, or are they repeatedly the last one picked for a team in gym class? Do you see them alone often? Have you seen people post strange or offensive things about them in group chats or on social media? Have you heard people gossiping about this person, in order to hurt them? Have you seen the person being verbally or physically abused? Is it one person who's doing the bullying, or is there a whole group involved? If you answered yes multiple times to the above questions, you can be pretty positive that person is being bullied.

Bullying can be extremely stressful and hurtful, and some victims have to seek professional help to cope with the trauma. It can cause a lot of long-term mental and physical problems, such as self-harm, eating disorders, suicidal thoughts, low self-esteem, trust issues, and so forth. So it's important to get a victim of bullying help right away.

But why do people bully? If you want to understand a bully's behavior, it can help you to learn more about the bully's background or home situation. There are many reasons why people bully, and it happens everywhere: in schools, at work, at home, on the playground, in the military . . . literally everywhere! A recent study by Ditch The Label (ditchthelabel.org) has shown that, contrary to what most people think, bullying does not happen because of who the victim is, or what they do, or what they look like. Bullying happens because bullies have issues of their own that they aren't dealing with. Here's some of the things bullies might be going through that can help explain (but not excuse) their behavior:

- **Stress and trauma:** We all respond to stress in different ways. Some of us use positive behaviors (meditation, therapy, sports) to reduce stress, while others use negative behaviors (bullying, violence, drugs). Some people simply don't know how to cope with stress at all.

- **They were bullied themselves in the past:** Bullying is often used as a defense mechanism and bullies start picking on people so that people won't pick on them.

- **They have a difficult home situation:** About 30 percent of all bullies feel their parents or guardians don't spend enough time with them on a daily basis. They feel rejected by the people who are supposed to love them unconditionally, and so they start behaving badly to get their attention.

- **They are insecure about relationships:** Bullies often feel like their closest friends and family aren't very supportive or loving.

You now know the most common reasons why bullies pick on others, but how can you help their victims? First of all, you tell victims of bullying that they are not alone. You might feel there isn't much you can do, but simply being there to support them can make a *huge* difference. Also, it might be a good move to involve some adults.

Are you afraid that your friend or relative is in danger from some bully? Report the bullying to an adult that you trust: a teacher, a parent, or a school counselor. There's a good chance they'll take action and inform the principal or the bully's parents. Although you're only trying to help them, be aware that the victim of the bullying might be really worried or ashamed that you told other people what's going on. They might even get angry with you for meddling in their business. Handle the situation with care and discretion, otherwise it might cause even more stress for the bullied person.

You can tell your friend or relative (or anyone you know who's being targeted by a bully) to join the DTL-community (Ditch the Label). DTL is one of the largest anti-bullying organizations in the world. They provide free access to expert help from one of their digital mentors, or you can post your questions or thoughts on the forum to get advice from people with similar experiences. All of it is anonymous, too, which is helpful for those who are afraid of being seen as weak.

But what if you're the bully? First of all, don't label yourself as a bully—it's not productive. Bullying is a behavior and not your identity, and yes, you can change your actions. Try to figure out why you bully others. Is there something going on in your life that you're reacting to? Once you understand what's causing your bad behavior, you can start to deal with the underlying problem.

Talk about your situation, whether it's with a friend, an adult you trust, or a professional counselor or therapist. You'll be surprised how empowering and liberating it can be just to sit with somebody you trust and tell them what's been eating at you. Remember that pulling someone else down is never going to raise you higher. Understand the impact of bullying: what you're doing can truly harm people and potentially scar them for life.

No matter which side of the situation you're on, we're all here to learn in this life, not to point fingers and judge. More than anything else, I'd like to advise you to seek the support you need both if you are being bullied or if you find yourself a bully to others.

You can find more on this topic on the following anti-bullying websites: http://www.antibullyingpro.com/useful-anti-bullying-websites/ and www.ditchthelabel.org. Some movies and series that taught me a lot about bullying were: *A Girl Like Her*, *Spijt!*, and *Audrie & Daisy*.

WHAT I ACTUALLY DO WHEN I SHOULD BE WORKING

KONCENTRATION

ACTUALLY WORKING (IF THIS IS HOW WORKING LOOKS)

WHAT I DO WHEN I SHOULD BE WORKING

PLAYING GAMES / CHECKING SOCIAL MEDIA

EATING OR SNACKING

STARING AND ANALYZING OTHER PEOPLE

DAYDREAMING (MOSTLY ABOUT FOOD)

STARING IN THE DISTANCE...

CHIT CHATTING WITH MY CO-WORKER

CREATING STUFF THAT HAS NOTHING TO DO WITH MY JOB

LISTENING TO MUSIC

TEN HACKS TO HELP YOU STOP PROCRASTINATING AND TO START DOING

It took me months of procrastination before I finally started writing this book. For weeks, I lay awake at night worrying that it wouldn't be finished on time. I dealt with a lot of stress and random panic attacks those last couple of weeks . . . and it was all because I waited too long to get to work on the writing and illustrating for the book. In the final months before my deadline, I started working like a lunatic in order to get everything done.

Why did I torture myself like that in the final weeks leading up to the deadline? I was given plenty of time to complete the project: all I had to do was write one chapter a month for about a year. I let it drag out so far that I had to write a chapter a week in order to get the manuscript done.

Is it because I like to work under pressure? Or am I just a lazy person? Do I enjoy the stress? Or am I just constantly making excuses for not writing?

The truth is: we all procrastinate sometimes. It's very easy to say, "I'll do that tomorrow," and then tomorrow becomes the day after tomorrow, and that becomes next week, and next week becomes never. We invent all kinds of creative excuses not to do what we're supposed to. What was your latest excuse for putting off exercising? Was it too cold, too hot, too humid, too tiring, too late? Or how about not completing a task like your homework or chores?

But we don't just postpone the small stuff. In fact, it's actually the bigger items on our to-do list that we tend to postpone the most, because they make us the most afraid of failing. Here are a few examples of scary things you might prefer to put off: big school assignments, dealing with fake friends, telling your crush that you like them, pursuing your dreams, or wanting a new job but being anxious to apply for one.

We constantly tell ourselves that today is not the right time. That might be true in some cases, but most often it's just an excuse to avoid taking a big leap. That's how our fears grow even larger, instead of smaller. And as time rolls by, our dreams and aspirations for "someday" remain exactly that: dreams and aspirations. You have to consider the possibility that someday might not come around in time, that perhaps you'll actually be too old, too financially unstable, or quite simply too late if you put off what you should be doing today.

Things we procrastinate the most on include:

- Exercising
- Cleaning
- Calling our family to see how they're doing
- Filing things, especially paperwork
- Asking someone out
- Studying for a test at school
- Apologizing to someone
- Keeping up with reading for school or work
- Answering letters or e-mails
- Investing or saving money for later
- Getting organized
- Learning a new language
- Getting to bed at a reasonable hour
- Trying new recipes
- Getting a different haircut

Some of the things above might seem like minor things, but they can still be examples of the fears I was talking about earlier. Anything related to work or school, no matter how small the individual task, can trigger your performance anxiety and make you afraid of imperfection or failure. Depending on how messy you are, the thought of organizing your things can seem overwhelming. If you put off handling your finances or making important decisions, this can indicate a fear of failure as well. If you procrastinate in confronting people, it might mean you're afraid of rejection or conflict.

Luckily, there's a number of very practical things that can help us get rid of our bad habit of procrastination. The rule of thumb is to live life *now*: don't wait until it's too late. It's all a matter of getting out of your comfort zone, really. Remember what we talked about in chapter 1? It can give us stress and anxiety to face things that are outside our comfort zone, but taking the plunge is the only way to expand your horizons. Mixing up your daily routine can be a very helpful way to stop procrastinating.

First of all, plan your tasks and deadlines. Whether they're for school, work, your hobby, your family, or your friends, you schedule that sh*t. Make an Importance/Urgency Matrix (see below). You can make a matrix for each part of your life, so you don't mix personal things with your school assignments. Stephen Covey (American businessman, keynote speaker, and author of the bestsellers *The 7 Habits of Highly Effective People* and *First Things First*) popularized the concept of a Time Management Matrix by suggesting the use of four quadrants. If you categorize your tasks according to their importance and urgency, you can easily see which one you need to do first. In other words, the matrix will tell you what your priorities are. Covey's matrix looks like this:

IMPORTANT AND URGENT: ACTUAL WORK (1)	NOT URGENT BUT IMPORTANT: ZEN WORK (2)
• Big School Project • Feeding the Cat • Seeing the Doctor	• Planning a Trip w/ the Girlfriends • Planning Some "Me Time" • Guitar Class
NOT IMPORTANT BUT URGENT: NAG WORK (3)	NOT IMPORTANT AND NOT URGENT: BUSY WORK (4)
• Texting My Sweetheart Constantly • Giving Attention to My Pet All the Time • Tagging My Bestie in All Those Memes	• Mindless Scrolling on the Web, TV • Checking Social Media, playing *The Sims* • Any Time-Wasting Activity, Like Having the Sudden Urge to Clean My Room Instead of Working on the Big School Project

The top left quadrant contains the most important and urgent tasks: those needing to be dealt with right now. In number two, on the top right, we find tasks that are important but not urgent. This is the quadrant that we should focus on if we want to achieve our long-term goals, according to Covey. In the bottom left we have a bunch of things that need to be eliminated or minimized. The tasks in this quadrant can be annoying because they take up a lot of your time and are mostly important to other people, not so much to you. The bottom right quadrant contains things that are not important and not urgent—they add no value to your work and are mostly a waste of your time.

This is an effective example of how you can organize your daily tasks and improve your productivity. Here are some other quick tips to help boost your productivity. Now stop procrastinating and start doing!

1. Set a deadline for each task. It doesn't matter how big or small the task is, if it doesn't have a due date, it's way too easy for you to put it off. Break the task or goal into smaller steps, which makes it easier and less overwhelming to start.

2. Visualize your goal. Put up pictures of the places you want to be able to travel to, the college you want to attend, someone you admire in the skill you want to master, and the like. Talk about your goals with others. Dress for the job you want instead of the job you have. Once you start believing that you're on your way to success, you have the positive mindset to get there.

3. Reward yourself for the progress you make. Sometimes you just have to treat yourself after a very productive day. Did you finish a big assignment? Well, good for you! You deserve a night out or a bowl of ice cream. If you set up a reward system to celebrate small achievements, you'll be able to do more in smaller steps. Before you even notice, you'll be one step closer to your goal.

4. There is no such thing as the right time. Step out of your comfort zone at least one a day. It doesn't really matter how fast you're going; what matters is that you *are going*. Whatever your

pace, you're already moving faster than anyone sitting on the couch at the moment.

5. The Ten-Minute Rule. This one is very effective for me. I tell myself I'll do something for just ten minutes—whether it's exercising or writing this book. This makes it easier to get started, and once I do, I always end up doing a full-body workout or a couple hours of writing. It feels so great and rewarding afterward having done more than the ten minutes I set out to do!

6. Do it for the rush you get afterward. The adrenaline, the kick, or the satisfaction you feel after you complete something is a reward in itself. It makes you feel so good about yourself and motivates you to keep going. And remember: no matter how much you've been procrastinating, it's never too late to get yourself together and make a start.

7. Focus on things that really matter, not just on low-hanging fruit or quick gains. I know this one's difficult. I used put a lot of time and energy into gaining more followers on social media, but now I focus my attention on my long-term work. I want to create things that'll be meaningful for a very long time, such as this book (Quadrant 2), instead of obsessing over my follower count or my next Facebook status (Quadrant 4).

HOW I FEEL AFTER NOT
PROCRASTINATING ONCE

8. Make it harder for yourself to procrastinate. If you do your homework in your room, it's very tempting to take a power nap instead. Keep your work and private life separate. Instead, go to the library, sit in the living room, or go to a café with your laptop. Or do your homework with a friend. You'll be more efficient and get the work done more quickly.

9. Visualize your timeline. Mark your deadlines on a calendar and use different colors for different tasks.

10. Prepare yourself before you get to work. You'll notice things go more smoothly if you've done your research and prep first. Put away the things that might distract you (such as your phone, games, TV), get your coffee or tea ready, and go, go, go!

WRITING A KICK-ASS RÉSUMÉ

A résumé is another term for a CV (*curriculum vitae*), which is a written compilation of your education, work experience, and accomplishments. Generally, you'll need this document (along with a cover letter) in order to apply for a job. A (short) job interview is usually also a part of the application process. Creating a *badass* résumé can help you in your search for the perfect job.

In your résumé, you basically try to sell yourself to an employer. Some people are too shy or afraid to put themselves out there and find it difficult to toot their own horns without feeling like a walking advertisement for themselves. Even the most outgoing people can have some trouble nailing it with a résumé. When it comes down to it, most applicants fail to be an eye-catcher for prospective employers. But a well-written résumé can be very persuasive, so if you do that right, you're far more likely to be invited for an interview. You'll even have a better shot than people who are more qualified than you but submitted a sucky résumé.

A good résumé tells everything about you professionally and academically, preferably in less than one page. Extra additions such as

Chrostin, 20 years old

skills:
· great at : memes
· not great at: being on time (sorry, I know)

About me:
I love cats so if you have something with cats, that would be awesome. I can surprise you now and then with being on time.

Please hire me ☺

Chrostin

examples of your work and a cover letter are not included in this one page. The first couple lines of your résumé are the most important, so you better make them count! Start by choosing a nice layout (there are many free templates available on the Internet if you don't know how to create your own). Don't make it look too plain, but don't overdo it, either. Find the right balance: makes sure it pops but is still easy to read.

Start by giving your personal information: your full name, (e-mail) address, phone number . . . all the factual data. Then proceed to list your skills, your academic history or current studies, and if there's room, your hobbies and interests. Those are the basic elements that make up a résumé. The following tips might come in handy if you want to stand out from the crowd and make your application extra awesome.

- If you're looking for a job that also includes working on or with the Internet, it's a good idea to link your (professional) websites and profiles, such as LinkedIn. You can add the websites of companies you've worked for in the past, or the school you went or are going to. Your current studies can be an advantage: they serve as proof of your social skills, as well as your writing and computer skills.
- Be specific and personal. Avoid using vague words to describe yourself, such as: *flexible, social, team player, hard worker, dynamic, motivated, go-getter*. In a résumé, everyone is suddenly flexible, very social, and a team player. Focus on the skills that are relevant to the job you're applying for, and use words like *created, launched, won, managed, trained, improved, got into, achieved*. An efficient way to do this is by using examples from your previous work or school experience.

Don't use: I'm creative.
Do use: I've worked for several brands (including X, Y, and Z) and created logos and website headers. I also illustrate and animate. You can find more of my work on my website (X) and my Instagram (Y).
Don't use: I'm a team player.
Do use: Having worked on several group projects at school, I've learned how to work on a team and delegate tasks. I'm more of a team leader, not a boss.
Don't use: I took part in an art competition once and did well.
Do use: Won Silver Medal at the (X) Live Art Competition in 2018.
Don't use: I got accepted into the XYZ University Communication Program.
Do use: I got accepted into the XYZ University Communication Program (7 percent admission rate, XYZ selects twenty-five students per semester).

- If you find it hard to describe your skills or strengths, ask your friends or family for feedback. They'll likely come up with qualities you didn't think of yourself or remind you of past accomplishments that you've forgotten. They can also help point out the obvious: things that you take for granted and forgot to mention because they're so, well, obvious.
- Be straightforward and honest. There's nothing more improper than lying about your skills or your past. Just because you listed the school(s) you went to doesn't mean the employer will automatically assume that you successfully completed the course or program. They'll need proof. True, some jobs don't require a degree, but if you lie about the school you went to or the degree you have, you might lose your chance of getting the job. If you haven't graduated yet, just be honest about it.

If you're in college, you can add your extracurricular activities and interests to increase the appeal of your résumé. Maybe you're into politics, history, or science fiction—you never know when your hobbies might come in handy. General knowledge and showing interest in different things make you an attractive applicant. If you already have an internship under your belt, specify your role there (for example, "communication intern at company X").

Proofread. If you've read your own CV multiple times, it's harder to catch a typo. It's a good idea to ask a few friends or relatives to proofread the document before you submit it. A typo or grammar mistake can be a deal breaker for some employers.

Update your résumé regularly. Add new experiences as you go along. Treat your résumé as a living document by adding new skills, courses you've taken, awards you've won . . . everything that might be relevant. Even if you already have a job, do it for future reference.

Get yourself out there! Send your résumé to multiple recruiters. Write them a professional e-mail, including a brief introduction, a short paragarph to explain why you want the job, and also include your awesome résumé as an attachment.

HOW TO STAND OUT WHEN APPLYING FOR A JOB

Applying for a (first) job is always very exciting. Student or part-time jobs are often limited in hours or short in duration, because you have to be at school on weekdays. The jobs are usually unrelated to what you're studying in school, and you should think of them as a way to earn some extra money, not a full salary. Here's some inspiration for part-time jobs: waiter/waitress, host(ess), bartender, barista, cashier, sales clerk, babysitter, after-school tutor, front desk associate, cleaner, ice-cream scooper, smoothie maker, library assistant, or maybe a paid intern (if you're a college student). I bet there are tons of options in your neighborhood.

I know that working part-time can be difficult while you're still in high school or college, and that's why you should look for the perfect job that fits your schedule. Here are some factors that you should keep in mind when you choose a job:

- **Make sure that the job is nearby, or at least easy to get to.** You don't want to stress yourself out about making it there on time or make a bad impression by arriving late.
- **Schedule your shifts according to your school hours.** Some jobs will require you to work mornings or nights, weekends or holidays. Make sure your school-work balance stays manageable. Don't bite off more than you can chew.
- **Find a job you like.** It's okay to have your eyes on the prize and to focus mostly on the pay when you look for a job. It'll earn you the money you need to go on a nice vacation or to buy yourself things. But try to choose a job you'll enjoy doing as well. You don't have to *love* it, but make sure you don't hate it. It'll be hard to stick with it if you dislike it.
- **Does the job help you with your future career?** If your part-time job is relevant to your professional area of interest, you're already a big step ahead. You could work as an intern for your favorite brand, start-up, or local business. The experience you'll build there might be very valuable at a later point in your career.

Now that you know what you should take into account, it's time to go job hunting! Where can you find a job? What are the dos and don'ts to survive your first job interview? Of course, not every part-time job requires a full-blown, lengthy interview. If you simply want to earn some extra money, you could look for a job that is easy to learn or doesn't require much experience or skills. However, if you're after a job that demands a bit more professionalism or might be a stepping stone to your dream career after graduation, keep on reading!

WHERE CAN I FIND A JOB?

Before you apply for a job, you'll obviously first need to find an opening that you're interested in. If you have some companies in mind that you'd like to work for, check their websites or social media pages to find out if they're hiring. Also, you can register with a temp agency or a recruitment agency: they'll get in touch with you if they have a job opening that might interest you. They usually have a database of positions waiting to be filled.

Social media is perfect for job hunting: Twitter, LinkedIn, Instagram, Facebook, etc. Just write a witty post to inform people that you're looking for a job—140 characters can be enough to convince someone to hire you!

Ask your friends or family if they know someone who needs an extra hand. They might be able to give you a heads-up when they learn about a new opening somewhere. Another great tip is to simply walk in to a company or store you are interested in and ask if they are hiring. That's how I found my first job as a waitress, and I kept it for over two years. Not every store or company will have a spot available, but this is still one of the most effective ways to find a job. Because it's ballsy and shows initiative!

THE JOB INTERVIEW: THE DOS AND DON'TS

If you're invited for an interview for a job you applied for (congrats!), you should be aware of some of the dos and don'ts of interviewing.

You totally should:

- **Prepare yourself.** Do lots of research about the company, the position, and the person who will be interviewing you. The more you know, the better your chances at getting the job.
- **Show up on time and with your best attitude.** Nothing is more

annoying to an employer than an applicant who shows up late for a first interview. It's downright rude and shows a lack of respect.

- **Give a firm handshake when you meet your interviewer.** A good handshake shows that you're confident, determined, and motivated. Make eye contact and smile from time to time while conversing with the interviewer. Sit up straight and look people in the eye.
- **Think before you answer.** A good technique is to give a brief summary of your answer first, and to elaborate on the individual points after. It's better to take your time to form a well-considered response than to rush. It's an interview, not a race!
- **Ask questions!** Inquiring about the job, the employer, or the industry itself shows that you're genuinely interested and eager to learn.

GOING TO A JOB INTERVIEW

DON'T

DO

WAKE UP 5MINS BEFORE THE INTERVIEW

LEAVE YOUR HAIR UNBRUSHED

COMB YOUR HAIR

BRUSH YOUR TEETH

GO WITH YOUR DRAGON BREATH

WEAR DIRTY CLOTHES

WEAR A PROPER OUTFIT THAT MAKES YOU FEEL COMFORTABLE

FIND A BALANCE BETWEEN SLAY AND CHILL

WEAR YOUR PAJAMAS

WEAR FILTHY SHOES

WEAR DECENT AND COMFY SHOES

WEAR YOUR LUCKY SOCKS

You totally shouldn't:

- **Drink, eat, or chew gum during the interview**. It's unprofessional and disrespectful.
- **Answer any calls or text messages.** Instead, leave your phone in your bag and put it on silent mode or shut it off completely.
- **Lie.** Lying won't get you anywhere. Give an honest answer to the questions you're asked, even if you have to admit you don't have the answer for something.
- **Show up wearing your leggings or jeggings.** Dress appropriately, because first impressions matter. I'm not saying you should wear a full three-piece suit, but your outfit should be in line with what the company is all about. Dress for the job you want. Wear clean clothes, brush your hair and your teeth, and make sure that you feel comfortable in what you are wearing.
- **Forget to breathe.** Stress can make you forget a lot of things, but you should never let your nerves take the upper hand. If you're nervous, do some breathing exercises before you go into the interview—it really helps! But be descreet about it—you don't necessarily want your interviewer to see how nervous you are.
- **Talk about irrelevant topics.** Potential employers don't expect you to talk about your love life or your religion. Keep it professional, unless you're asked about other stuff. Making a joke is allowed, but don't overdo it.

Bonus Tips for Standing Out Among Other Candidates

- Give plenty of examples to highlight your previous work experience and list some of the things that interest you outside of school, such as blogging, writing music, leading a sports team, coaching, tutoring, etc.
- Write a thank-you letter or e-mail within twenty-four hours of your interview. Tell the recruiters you're looking forward to hearing from them, that you enjoyed your conversation, and that you look forward to the next steps.

- Don't forget to start and finish by explaining *why* you want the job. Recruiters want to see passion and eagerness.
- Be yourself. There's no need to be somebody else. Employers will hire you for who you are, not for who you want to be.

WHEN YOUR PASSION AND YOUR PARENTS' WISHES DON'T MIX

All parents want their kids to be successful. Every time your parents give you the "doctor-lawyer-engineer" lecture, try to remember that they mean well—they want you to have a successful career and an amazing future. But what if your dream doesn't involve becoming a doctor, lawyer, or engineer? What if you're passionate about something else? What if you want to become an artist? What if you want to grow up to be the next Shakespeare or to star in a Netflix original series? What if you have no clue what you want to be yet, you just know what you *don't* want to be? Wherever you're at, the important thing here is how to tell your parents that you don't see yourself in a white coat with a stethoscope around your neck, or sitting at a desk behind a nameplate that reads CEO.

At first, you might feel as if your parents won't let you choose what you want to be. You might get some resistance from them, but that's mostly because they worry about you and want to protect you. It's their job; they can't help it. Also, it can be a little scary for them to watch you make your own decisions and find your own path in life. On top of that, they might also feel regret or envy because they never got to chase their dreams when they were younger. Remember that the world was a different place when your parents were your age; back then it wasn't as easy for young people to follow their passions as it is now.

I grew up in a middle-class family of laborers. My dad and grandma worked at the national postal service, my granddad was a technician at a hospital, and my mom, who had been a singer in her home country, worked as a cleaning lady. So, they did nothing fancy or high ranking, I would say. They all just worked really hard to earn enough money to feed the family. But that's why my brother and I feel enormous pressure to succeed in life. In our family, we are the first ones to continue our education after high school. My mom never got the chance to study in her home country, so it's really important to her that we do so. She never got the chance to fully develop herself or get a degree, so she wants to make sure that we do.

I was never too sure—I still am not—about what I wanted to be when I grew up. As a child, I wanted to be a vet, a professor, or a teacher. Later, I wanted to be a weather reporter. I changed my mind a lot, but I was always sure about one thing: I didn't want to study for it. Without knowing what I *really* wanted, I finished high school and began studying communication management in college right after. Maybe I could've traveled for a year first? Studied abroad? Learned a new skill? Or I could've just started working, as I knew even before I started that studying wasn't the right thing for me. In the end, I enjoyed my years in college, although I knew from the beginning that I didn't want to work in the communications field. That's partly because I'm still figuring out what one actually does with a degree in communications, but also because part of me wants to become a full-time artist.

The arts (and there are other examples, including many of the humanities) are still not fully accepted as a profession, and people often think of them as hobbies, not careers. "Find a real job" and "you'll need a degree anyway" are only a few of the prejudices I have to deal with as an artist. Many people are biased and quick to think that art can't be a full-time job, unless you make it big as an artist. It was never my dream to become a professional artist, or a writer, or both. And that's mainly because no one ever told me that those were actual options. I didn't know I could do that! So becoming a full-time illustrator was more like a pipe dream.

My dream was to make my parents proud, because I was the first in our family to go to college. My mom always wanted me to become a teacher, but I soon ruled out that option. It just wasn't for me. One time in high school, I had the crazy idea to switch to an art school in a different city. I was young and influenced by the wild enthusiasm of my friend, who desperately wanted to go herself. I wasn't allowed to go, of course, and the plan soon slipped to the back of my mind. I kept going to a drawing academy once a week instead. It wasn't the same, but I understood why my parents didn't let me switch schools. I hadn't thought through why I wanted to go. I was only fourteen or fifteen at the time and not ready to commute to another city by myself every day. I also didn't discuss the option properly with my parents. I just sprung it on them and that didn't go over so well. And I couldn't honesty answer the question as to why I wanted to go. Did I want to go for myself or simply for my friend?

If you're considering something similar at the moment, I'm not implying that you haven't thought about your decision enough; I'm just saying that *I* did not. However, you should really think it through, and you should feel completely ready and motivated before you make a move. Also, make sure you do it for you, not because your friends are doing it.

The most important tip I can give you is to start communicating with your parents up front about your goals and your aspirations. Open up honestly to them. Perhaps they'll be hesitant at first. "Will you earn any money doing this job? Can you make a living doing this?" will likely be foremost on their minds and you should be prepared to answer these questions. Your parents want you to be comfortable, happy, and successful as an adult. Maybe they want your life to be easier and better than theirs. In the end, I don't think they really care *what* you become; they just want you to have the life you want and to be making the right choice for you.

Essentially, your parents just want you to be happy. Great, so do you, and you want them to be happy, too. If you talk about your plans openly with them, they'll eventually understand and be proud of you for your choices. Also, try to make them see that sometimes it's better to regret the things you've done in life than the things you never tried.

THAT FIRST PAYCHECK IS OH SO SWEET

I remember being fourteen and getting my first summer job, which meant I also got my first paycheck. I wasn't saving for anything in particular, but I knew that I wanted to be more independent from my parents. I wanted to buy myself some cute clothes, candy, and movie tickets. But what if you really have no clue what to do with the money you're earning in your part-time job? If you have a steady income (because you work every week or during school vacations), you might be saving for something that requires a lot of money (such as a trip, your tuition, or even a tattoo), or maybe you just want some extra spending money, like I did.

When I got my first *real* job at nineteen, I worked as a freelance illustrator for a Belgian magazine. I remember receiving my first legit salary and the amount was so huge to me, I didn't even know what to do with it. I ended up buying a professional drawing tablet, which was an investment in a way. Two years later, I still use that same drawing tablet.

There's no "best way" to spend your first salary or paycheck. It all depends on your situation and what you want to spend it on. Getting your first paycheck is a very special moment, though, and almost everyone remembers what they bought with the money.

Here are a few meaningful ways you could use it:
- **Save it, or at least a part of it.** This paycheck is a milestone and the start of your financial freedom is something special!
- **Buy something.** Yes, buy something! Treat yourself. Do it yourself and pay for it with your own cash or debit card. The feeling of independence is truly great and the novelty of it will wear off soon,

so you better enjoy the rush now. Make sure you don't overdo it with the spending, though, unless you're sure you'll save more the next time.

- **Pay back any loans or debts.** Have you borrowed money from people recently? Time to pay them back (preferably with a thank-you note, too).

- **Help someone else.** Whether it's buying food for someone in need or donating to a charity, give something back. You have the luxury of being able to afford food, clothes, and nice things, but there are so many people out there who can't make ends meet. Donating even a small amount can make a big difference.

- **Buy something for your parent(s).** Give them something special, something they deserve for taking care of you for so long. You're growing up, and getting your first paycheck is a big part of becoming financially independent. Time to say thanks.

- **Invest.** Think about getting life insurance or putting money in a Roth IRA or mutual fund. Although you're very young and probably not particularly interested in taxes, insurance, and the like, getting insurance or investing is a smart move. The younger you are, the more affordable these things are.

Chapter Eight

{ THE INTERNET OF THINGS }

We spend a lot of time online: checking social media, reading the news, shopping for favorite brands, watching TV or online series. This is all made possible on the awesome interwebs. But as beautiful as the Internet is, it can a dangerous place, too, if you're not careful.

MILLENNIALS' BIGGEST ADDICTION: THE SMARTPHONE?

When I was in my final year of college, we had a course called Communication Research. For our final oral exam, we were allowed to discuss a topic of our choice, and I picked "Cell Phone Addiction in Youngsters." For research, I read a study (which was rather old) on why adolescents feel the need to check their phones constantly.

Why is it, exactly, that we can't seem to put our smartphones down? And how bad does it have to be before we're truly addicted? Is it even possible to become addicted to technology? Can we really compare phones to drugs like alcohol or weed? The answer to all of the above is yes, but it's even more difficult to notice and to know where to draw the line. Also, people underestimate the effects of a phone addiction on them and their well-being.

Our smartphone has become an important part of our daily lives. We use it every day to call, chat, text, or check social media. We even keep it by our bedside at night. Even when we are spending time with our friends or family, it has become completely normal to answer phone calls or return texts almost immediately. Why do we feel the need to answer these texts or to check our social media feeds constantly, even while we are in the company of our friends and family?

The line between overuse and addiction is very thin. Dr. David Greenfield, founder of the Center for Internet and Technology Addiction, confirms that many people overuse their smartphones. According to him, you are moving into addiction territory if you can't stop using your phone, even when you know it's ruining (parts of) your life. If you can't help being on your phone, even when you know you really shouldn't be, that lack of control is an important sign of addiction, he concludes.

You've probably read some articles on how your phone's blue light can keep you awake at night or how social media can make feel sad or depressed. There are a bunch of psychological effects related to smartphone addiction, including the following:

• **Sleep disturbance:** The bright light from your smartphone or tablet screen can decrease your sleep quality. It can take you longer to fall asleep because your brain is still active from the light of your screen.

• **Relationship problems:** As your online connections grow and flourish, your offline relationships might suffer. It's possible that you're neglecting the people you interact with in real life as a result of your excessive cell phone and social media use.

- **Anxiety:** Research has shown that college students who use their phones a lot are more likely to feel anxious and restless in their downtime.
- **A bunch of physical effects** can also be added to this list: eye fatigue, itchy or burning eyes, neck problems (notice how you're constantly looking down at your phone, tablet, or computer), and so on. There's also an increased risk of car accidents caused by texting and driving, which can be just as dangerous and deadly as drinking and driving!

Breaking the Phone Addiction

If you find yourself checking your phone first thing in the morning—before even getting out of bed—you might have a serious problem. Get rid of this habit by starting your day in a healthy way. Try to get out of bed immediately, stretch, drink a glass of water, meditate, and eat a healthy breakfast without looking at your phone. Try it and you'll feel so much fresher during the day. Your phone shouldn't be a part of your morning routine.

Part of the problem is that we have our phone with us almost constantly. The only time we're not checking our besties' Facebook statuses is when we're taking a shower. We find ourselves mindlessly passing time by touching our screens, even when we should be doing homework or other productive things. In fact, we're constantly distracted by the ringing, buzzing, beeping, and pinging of our phones. The result? Your focus is completely gone and you're getting absolutely zero work done. The solution? Create phone-free zones and times throughout your day. For example: if you do your homework between 4:00 and 6:00 p.m., completely shut down your phone and focus on the task in front of you. Also create a no-phone zone, such as the living room or your bedroom, especially in the last two hours before bed-time. Also, don't leave your phone under your pillow while you sleep! This can be very dangerous for two reasons: radiation and explosion.

We somehow feel the urge to be connected to the outside and Internet *all the time*. When we aren't, we instantly experience FOMO: the fear of missing out. You think you're missing out on all the important stuff that's happening in the online world, while actually, your life is happening right now. If you find yourself texting, checking Facebook, or tweeting while you're having a conversation with someone, you should know that's kinda rude. Even if everybody's doing it. It breaks down friendships and can ruin your relationships with others. Your behavior implies that the virtual message you're replying to, which can totally wait in 99.9 percent of all cases, is more important than the person in front of you. Leave your phone at home, or put it on "do not disturb" mode so you'll get zero beeps from new notifications while you are with a friend or your family.

Another way of measuring how addicted to your phone you are is how anxious you feel if you don't have it with you. Do you feel uncomfortable, ill at ease, or even terrified if your phone is out of sight? Do you feel more comfortable when you feel your phone in your pocket, not because you need it, but just because you know it's there?

If you answered yes to the above, then try a digital detox. Go without social media or your phone for at least a whole day, preferably even a week. When you go back online, you'll notice that the notifications you received in your absence weren't life-changing at all. Heck, most of the time when you take out your phone, it's not even because someone has actually called or texted you; rather, you're just constantly waiting for something to happen—a message, a notification, more likes on a post. After a digital detox, you'll realize how unimportant social media is. Repeat it regularly, and you'll smell the flowers and hear the birds singing again. There's more to life than the digital world, trust me.

Try to imagine how people got by twenty years ago. I think I'm part of one of the last generations born into a world without smartphones and tablets. Honestly, I'm not saying that things were necessarily better back then, but they were very different for sure.

Writing and sending love letters was the norm, not the exception. We played outside more often than kids do today. While we were growing up, Internet technology started to boom. In my teenage years, we used MSN Messenger and Netlog. Suddenly, we were taking pictures of ourselves and posting them (the word *selfie* hadn't even been invented yet) and creating an online persona.

Of course, technology has made our lives easier and more efficient in many ways. We live at a very high speed and the online information-flow never stops. That's why it's hard for us to keep up with everything, and it's also why we feel left out whenever we can't check our social media for a while. But the sooner we realize that the offline world is the *real* world, where the *real* stuff happens, the sooner we'll be able to get rid of this twenty-first-century addiction.

THE TRUTH ABOUT VIRTUAL FRIENDS

The top locations for teens to hang out with their friends are school, someone's house, or online. Now that technology is everywhere, it has become so much easier to meet friends and even lifelong partners on the Internet. Social media, online video games, and fandom sites have made it easy to interact with awesome people around the world who share the same interests as you. In all honesty, it's a lot easier to start a conversation online than in real life—especially with someone you might like or want to hang out with. And if it doesn't work out, it's not like you have to see that person anywhere, ever.

Your physical friends can't be around you 24/7. And we get a lot of updates on their lives on social media, too. Having virtual friends *can* be much better than having friends in real life, because you met in a virtual place where you both ended up because you're interested in the same thing. In that way you have a connection on a different level. The Internet allows us to talk to people we *want* to associate with. There's no social structure, like a school or club, that forces us to interact with these people, and the Internet isn't interested in labeling us or putting us into boxes.

For example, it only takes a few seconds to find someone who's an equally huge fan of your idol as you are. And the beautiful thing is, they're not ashamed to openly express their fandom on the Internet. In real life, depending on how "cool" your idol is, that can be a lot more difficult to do. In the virtual world, you're able to express yourself to an online community of people who understand what you're saying. Virtual friends can make you feel more confident, loved, and appreciated than some "real" people.

When it comes to keeping in touch, virtual friendships can be a little different from real-life friendships. Your virtual friend might live on the other side of the planet, and there you have the first problem: time zones. You'll have to find a moment when you're both awake and have a moment to talk to keep each other updated. Obviously, you don't have to go through all that trouble with your real-life friends. But if your online friendship makes you happy and satisfies your social needs, isn't it worth it? You can still talk to each other almost every day, share inside jokes, and send each other memes and songs to keep your digital friendship alive. You can even think about visiting them, wherever they live—a new adventure for you to share together, in real life!

A friend is someone who cares for you, remembers your birthday, and offers a shoulder to cry on. If you feel like someone you've met online could provide you all of these things and more, it's only a matter of time before you're going to want to meet each other in real life. If you both want to, you can move your friendship from the virtual world to the real one. You might even fall in love, too. If you do decide you want to meet your virtual friend, though, you should be extra careful: you *never* really know for sure who's on the other side of your screen, even if you've called or Skyped them before. It's believed by many that people are less genuine online than in real life, so always keep in mind that you might be in for a disappointment, or even worse: a trap. Make sure that, when you're meeting up in real life, you feel comfortable enough. Maybe it's a good idea to meet in a group first. Or at least in a public area like a coffee shop or a shopping mall. Also, always let a parent or a friend know where you're going and who you are going to meet. Remember: you're seeing a stranger for the very first time and you should make sure that you're safe.

But I'm not here to make you afraid of online relationships. They can be really great, and some might turn into lifelong friendships. I've met so many interesting and awesome people through social media, and I never would've known them if I wasn't active online. Some of them became real friends that I trust deeply. Thanks to the Internet, it's easier to chat with Chrostin fans, too. And I can send messages to my own idols without having to look up their address to write them a fan letter. Sometimes they respond and that's an awesome feeling! We are literally a few clicks away from each other.

Despite the fact that we are less likely to meet our virtual friends in real life, they can sometimes be closer to us than our real-life friends. Some teens simply don't feel comfortable talking face-to-face and prefer chatting online. In terms of sharing thoughts and communicating, both offline and online friendships are equally valuable. However, if most of your social interactions take place online, you might get so used to expressing yourself through texting and chatting that you forget how to communicate with people in the real world. Make sure you don't forget how to have an old-fashioned, real-life conversation! If you don't interact with people in real life, you'll lose out on developing some important communication skills that you'll need in order to deal with all kinds of situations. For example, confronting someone face-to-face is a whole different ball game compared to doing so online. Make sure you don't put yourself at a disadvantage by letting your real-life social skills become all rusty.

ONLINE DATING DOS AND DON'TS

It's super easy to lie about who you are on the Internet. Pictures that aren't yours can easily become yours; all you have to do is post them and claim ownership over them. You can pretend to be a teenage boy or girl, even if you're actually a grown man or woman with bad intentions. This phenomenon is called *catfishing*: actively tricking someone into believing you're someone else. A catfish will invest incredible amounts of time into creating a backstory that seems legit and will go through any amount of trouble to gain their victim's trust. Once the trust is earned, it's super easy to set a date to meet face-to-face. You might be tempted to meet up with people you've met online in secret, without telling your parents or friends. This can be incredibly dangerous; even if they *are* the person in the pictures they sent you, you still don't know what their intentions might be.

To avoid this kind of situation, I've listed the dos and don'ts of teenage online dating here:

DON'T:

- be careless about giving away your private information. No person on the Internet should know your personal details. Keep your full name, address, location, and other private details to yourself.
- meet up in a private place. That's asking for problems, really. It's only okay to meet up at a private place if you know each other well enough *and* if other people are aware of your whereabouts.
- send nude pictures that include your face. Obviously, it's best if you don't send any nude pics at all, for many different reasons, but if you choose to do so, never include your face so that no one can recognize you on the photos. Also, try to make the environment of the photo less distinct so that people can't identify your location. Always be aware of the potential consequences of the pictures you send over the Internet. Remember that everything you put online can be traced and shared.
- send money to someone you only know on the Internet. You never know what they're going to use the money for, and there's a good chance they'll scam you just to get more money.
- engage if the other person wants you to do stuff that you don't like. This could be anything. You have the right to say no, and if the person you're talking to doesn't understand or respect that, that's an obvious red flag.
- pretend to be someone you're not. Honesty is the best policy in online dating. After all, you also want the other person to be honest with you.
- ever give away your passwords to your social media accounts (or any other password for that matter).
- push the other person too much if they don't reply to your message(s) immediately. Remember that the other person doesn't *have* to answer you right away. Perhaps they're thinking about what to write back, or maybe they simply forgot about it. If you sense that they might have lost interest, accept this as well and chat with other people.

DO:

- stay true to yourself online. It's okay to show a better version of yourself, but don't feed people false information to make yourself look better or more interesting. The person has to like you for who you are, not for who you pretend to be.
- tell an adult about your Internet date if you decide to meet up in real life.
- find out if you and your online crush have the same values and opinions on important issues, or at least make sure you'll have stuff to talk about in real life.
- meet up in a public space. That could be any place where other people can see the two of you: a café, a movie theater, a restaurant, a local park, etc.
- warn someone if you feel uncomfortable. Always have someone on hand in case your date turns out to be a complete weirdo and you want to leave ASAP! Remember that you never ever have to stay anywhere you don't feel like staying.
- create a music playlist to tell the other person how you feel.
- use the right amount of emojis. They can make a message so much more fun!
- unfriend the person if you don't feel comfortable dating anymore. It's okay to block them if you feel that your privacy or your safety is in danger.

Looking for a safe way to date online as a teenager? There are no guarantees when you talk to people online, but there are a few tips on how to stay as safe as possible in the digital world. Avoid chat systems like Chatroulette, Chatrandom, and Omegle. Those apps connect you to strangers all over the world and are especially tricky because they offer a video chat option. It's highly unlikely that you'll find the love of your life on one of these systems, as most of the visitors on there are adult men looking for young boys and girls, nudity, and explicit conversations. Just saying: there are better platforms out there.

Here are some alternatives to "adult" dating apps like Tinder, Grindr, and more "serious" dating websites:

- **Spotafriend:** Allows teen and tweens to swipe on profiles, get pictures and connect with nearby strangers. They claim they're not a dating app, but a way to make new friends. Spotafriend describes itself as an app for people aged thirteen to nineteen.

- **MyLol:** Aimed at teenagers for social networking and dating. You have to be at least thirteen to be on this app, and no older than nineteen. Be aware of predators regardless of those age restrictions. The app recently received a low rating from Common Sense Media because of the large number of explicit photos circulating on there.

- **Yubo:** An app for teenagers thirteen and up. Yubo (formerly Yellow) is often described as the "Tinder for Teens," because the system is the same (with the swiping and all). Be careful, though, because there is no age verification system included in the app.

- **MeetMe:** A famous online flirting and social networking app with over one million active users. The app requires access to your geolocator, so be mindful of who you match with, as they can see where you are.

- **Skout:** Pretty much the same system as MeetMe, as it uses your phone's GPS to connect to people nearby. Due to increased moderation, this might be one of the safest options. For example, it's not possible to send pictures in private conversations, and people can't see your precise location, either, only a general region.

Of course, it's not up to me to tell you what you can and can't do when it comes to dating, but I can at least inform you about the safest options. As a teenager who grew up using the beta versions of these kinds of apps, I can honestly tell you that online dating is exciting, fun, and inspiring, *if* you do it safely. Meeting new people is great but can be dangerous, too. If you're looking for someone in your neighborhood to date, try to remember the dos and don'ts from the lists on previous page. And have fun! If you want more information on dating and sex, read all about it in chapter 6.

ONLINE CONFLICTS: WHAT ARE THEY AND HOW TO DEAL WITH THEM

Even online, where people are relatively safe behind their phone or computer screen, it's not uncommon to run into some pretty weird or unpleasant situations, and cyberbullying is one of them. Someone might make nasty comments about you or someone else you know based on your online photos or profiles. This can give you anxiety or stress, and it can be very upsetting to read. Cyberbullying is a very serious issue and should never be ignored or left unchallenged. It can be just as bad as real-life bullying in terms of psychological consequences. On top of that, it can be very difficult to find who's behind the bullying, because the Internet makes it super easy to stay anonymous and to fly under the radar.

There are many forms of cyberbullying—here are five common types. The important thing for you to do is understand how cyberbullying happens, how you can recognize the sings, and what you can do about it.

1. Online Stalkers

Ever since Chrostin got her own Instagram page, her following grew slowly but steadily. Most of her fans were young, female, and were interested in Chrostin because they enjoy the witty comics. By *most*, I mean 93 percent of all Chrostin's followers. I felt great about having created my own safe space online. But then, completely out of the blue, some men started to message me, addressing me personally. Theoretically, there is nothing wrong with that, as my page is also meant for men who appreciate my comics. But the tone of their messages changed after I replied. At first, I was friendly and accepted the compliments they gave me, but I also kept a firm distance. I was never trying to be anything more than simply polite; I wanted to avoid being mean or dismissive, as most of them probably didn't mean any harm. Unfortunately, some of them mistook my politeness for flirtation and started to message me more and more for no apparent reason. They told me that I looked pretty today, that I was mesmerizing, that my smile was beautiful, that I reminded them of some character from a computer game (don't ask, that was just plain creepy), and many more things. At first, I didn't see any problem with this. A compliment never hurt anybody, right?

Right. But a compliment is a compliment, and stalking some-one on a daily basis is something else. There was this one guy in particular—let's call him Alex. Alex lived in New York and noticed that I was visiting the city for business. Alex talked to me a lot online, and I tried to reply as often as I could. When he started to push me to hang out with him when we were both in New York, that was a huge red flag to me. I was in Brooklyn for a photoshoot, and as I posted some Instastories about the shoot, he continuously messaged me to tell me how "jaw dropping" I looked. For the record: the photoshoot was for the author photo for this book. It was 23 degrees outside, and I was literally wearing a turtleneck and long trousers. And even if I *had* been wearing a more showy outfit, that still wouldn't have given him the right to harass me like that. A male friend of mine even thought the situation was frightening, because Alex constantly wanted to know where I was and desperately wanted to know why we couldn't hang out.

I ended up telling Alex that he was being creepy and stalky, to which he replied that it was a joke and not intended that way. Right. A joke. None of it was a joke until I called him out on it. His desire to meet me. His creepy intentions. His stalky behavior and constant inquiries to find out where I was. None of that was a joke, at least not to me. After the confrontation, I blocked him from my page so that he couldn't see anything new I posted. Unfortunately, he wasn't the first and he won't be the last person I encounter who has a weird stalker vibe. The moral of this story is that you should never stay polite to someone who tries to invade your privacy or personal space. If they make you feel weird or uncomfortable, take it as a warning sign that you should take action. Luckily for me, I didn't respond to his invitations to meet, because my instinct told me it wasn't a good idea to meet up with a strange man in a country I'd never visited before in my life.

Unfortunately, online stalking is not a new phenomenon and it happens every day to countless teenagers around the world. Social media has made it really easy to create fake accounts and to pretend to be someone else in order to get things from another person: talking about private stuff, blackmailing, chatting, sharing private information or explicit photos, meeting up, and so on.

If you are confronted with this kind of behaviour in any way, please speak up. If someone stalks you or harasses you online, tell a friend or an adult. Tell them you feel uncomfortable with the way that person talks to you. In some cases, involving a parent or other adult you trust can be enough to scare the stalker away. Other times, the stalker might be more persistent and not give up so easily. Of course, being stalked is never fun, but there are a few practical things you can do to handle the situation (or to prevent it):

- Adjust your privacy settings on social media. Allow friends and family only to see your profile and what you post. This might seem like an obvious tip, but teens nowadays seem to be less aware of online privacy. On Twitter, you can always shield your tweets from general public viewing. The same goes for Instagram, Snapchat, and Facebook; decide how public you want your accounts to be, but be mindful—if you throw your stuff out there for everyone to see, it's almost unavoidable to have some creeps staring at your summer vacay pics. I know, I should be the first to openly admit that having social media accounts with a relatively big following isn't always the most private way to socialize. That's why I also created a private account: the 700 followers I have on there are peanuts compared to the 50K followers on my public Instagram account. On my private (meaning: locked) account, I share my selfies and other more trivial and personal content. That's because I don't feel the need for my followers to know every little detail about my private life, and it's my way to keep the creeps away.

- **Block, report, and delete.** If a Facebook friend bothers you, don't feel sorry for them; just delete them. Preferably block them, too, so there is no way they can view your profile online again. If someone is stalking you anonymously, report it to Facebook right away so their account gets shut down. The same steps apply to followers on Instagram, Snapchat, or Twitter.

- **Mute the Instagram comments.** With this feature, you can mute the comments section of your Instagram page. Then, if the harassment or bullying won't stop, at least you're not confronted with it.

- **Document everything.** Tweets, statuses, posts, messages, and all can be deleted or taken down at any time. Make sure to take screenshots, save links, and remember the (screen) names of the stalkers. If the stalking gets out of hand, at least you'll have evidence of the harassment so you can provide that to the police if necessary.

- **Be careful with the geo-tag.** A geo-tag is the link to your location, and it's your choice to share it or not. Teens think of it as a fun feature to let their friends know where they are and what they're doing at the moment. They often forget that, if their profile is public, *everyone* can see where they are and who they are with. It's a very easy way for predators to locate young teens without being noticed.
- **Never ever give away private information online**—not yours, not someone else's. That includes phone numbers, private e-mail addresses, physical addresses, where somebody works, and so forth.

If none of this is enough, and the harassment continues, call the police and get them up to speed on the situation. Stalking can be a very serious and scary matter, and if you feel that your privacy or your life might be in danger, don't ignore your instincts. Tell a trusted adult and be sure to protect yourself.

Suggested further reading: *The Smart Girl's Guide to Privacy: A Privacy Guide for the Rest of Us* by Violet Blue.

2. Social Media Fights

Have you ever been involved in a social media fight? Or at least seen one? In the years I've been active on social media, I've witnessed my fair share of online fights. Whether it's between celebrities or between people I vaguely know, it's always kind of exciting and entertaining. But what if you're a part of the fight? And why do so many fights happen on social media anyway?

Many online debates or fights start because someone (or multiple people) disagrees with something you've posted online. It can be a picture, a tweet, a post, a status . . . that other person might feel the need to tell you you're wrong publicly, or they might want to tell you that they take offense to what you posted. Then come the comments, and things often start to heat up from that point. Mean things are being said and personal attacks are being launched. At this point, more people (who have nothing to do with the fight) will likely get involved in the argument, either to rush to the defense of the person they think is right or to harass the other party.

Whatever you do, try not to add fuel to the social media fight fire and try not to engage with the haters who are attacking you. If things get personal, it's only because the other person/people are interested in hurting you, not in having a mature debate. If you all want to have a proper discussion, be respectful of each other and add legitimate, valid arguments. Online fights usually blow over really quickly and tomorrow they'll be old news. Every decision you make during the argument, however, can impact the course of the fight. Own up to things you said earlier; deleting posts won't make the issue go away. It can even make things worse because it makes you look a little weak, like you're admitting that you were wrong. Also, remember that people take screenshots faster than they blink, so even if you do delete a post, it could very likely be added as photographic evidence against you later.

I was caught in the middle of a social media storm once while I was working for a magazine in Belgium. A competing famous magazine—I'll leave their name out of the story—stole a joke/comic that I had made a few hours prior to their post. Of course, I was furious, because their post was a big success and for me, as a beginning illustrator, that was exposure that could've helped me a lot. In my rage, I wrote a blog post to vent about how difficult it was for a small fish like me to compete with a large company like theirs. Instead of giving me a credit for the comic, they took down the post and sent me a letter of apology via e-mail, which was a victory to me. But it didn't end there. In the meantime, people had started accusing me of plagiarism and being an attention seeker. People I didn't even know started to attack me personally and told me I didn't have a sense of humor and sucked at drawing. What did all of that even have to do with my blog post? You guessed it—nothing.

I left my phone alone for a whole day and night, because I wanted things to calm down a bit. Of course, I was freaking out on the inside, but I figured it wasn't the best idea to get more deeply involved in this fight with people I didn't even know. In social media fights, it's best to keep the conversation between you and the other person as much as possible without responding to any third parties who get involved later.

Surviving your first online battle will automatically make you more careful about what you tweet or post in the near future, but prevention is always best. Before you share anything on social media, ask yourself the following questions about your post:

• Could it affect me, my friends, or my reputation?
• What would my parents or friends think if I posted this?
• Will I stand by my opinion, no matter what?

Remember: social media is a tricky beast and there are no guarantees that what you post, however inoffensive you think it to be, won't come under attack by an online troll. No matter how innocent and harmless your post, there's always a chance you'll get caught in a sh*tstorm you didn't see coming. People have different opinions and perspectives on life, so they might interpret your tweet, post, or status differently than you intended. Don't let this hold you back, and don't be afraid to post and share whatever you like. The unpredictability of social media can be a beautiful thing, too: strangers on the Internet might surprise you by giving you compliments or by telling you they couldn't agree more with what you're saying. Just know that when posting something, you are putting yourself out there and must be ready for anything to happen.

3. Online Trolls

A *troll* is Internet slang for someone who starts arguments or tries to upset people by posting irrelevant or off-topic messages on a forum, blog, online community, or chat room. Their only intention is to provoke an emotional response from people who read their post, just for the troll's own entertainment. In recent years, the concept of trolling has become more and more associated with online harassment. Trolls enjoy getting under people's skin and feed off their anger, disgust, and outrage. Like circus clowns, Internet trolls hide behind anonymous accounts and fake usernames. That makes it even more difficult to trace the person behind the harassment.

EHM... YOU'RE*

* TYPING *

Annoyingly, trolls are all over the Internet. You'll find them on any site that offers an open comment section where people can freely express their thoughts and opinions. Getting rid of them is hard, because there are so many people on the Internet and it's impossible to control what everyone writes. Blocking, deleting, or banning a troll can be a good first step, as well as reporting that person or account to the site administrator or moderator. If it's your own website or blog that is the victim of a troll, you could simply close off the comments section.

Trolls come in all shapes and sizes, and they all have their own particular reason for trolling. Most of them do it only for the sake of trolling, but others might have different intentions. Here are a few types of trolls to be on the lookout for:

- **Hate Speech Troll:** Targets people based on prejudice, including women, people of color, religious people, LGBTQIA+ people, etc.
- **Cyberbully Troll:** A general troll with no specific target. This type of troll simply hates on everyone by calling them names and insulting them.

- **Argument Troll:** Always want the last word and won't budge until others give up. Usually slaps you around the ears with statistics, scientific studies, and links to websites to prove a point.
- **Grammar Nazi Troll:** Feels the need to rub people's noses in it when they make a spelling mistake or grammatical error on an online post or article. They'll correct the offending mistake or sentence with an asterisk symbol and add a sneering comment. They draw attention away from the actual topic and use the editorial mistakes as a way to undermine the other person's argument.
- **Griefing Troll:** This phenomenon comes from the online gaming world. It's used to describe a group of players who create a bunch of free accounts, and then gang up on and attack a single player to ruin their gaming experience. In a broader context, griefing happens when a lot of people each put in a minor effort, such as posting a hateful tweet, to create a big, cumulative effect. One hateful tweet is easy to ignore, but if you receive fifty of them in quick succession, the effect could be horrible.

Of course, there are many more types of online trolls, but the ones mentioned are the most common. Trolls like to "flame" people, meaning to verbally attack them online. Flaming can take the form of name-calling or insulting and is directed at a specific person. Topics such as politics, abortion, immigration, racism, religion, or anything LGBTQIA+-related are typical triggers for flaming attacks. A frequent flamer is definitely an Internet troll.

Trolls are like demons; they feed on negative energy. And so they push random people's buttons and fire insults at them to get a reaction. They place themselves outside of the social order, meaning they don't hold themselves accountable because they think social rules don't apply to them. They find it amusing when the person they are attacking gets angry or upset with them. So how can you defeat an online troll?

Well, you certainly won't win by playing their game. Trolls are childish attention seekers who enjoy drama and quick-fire emotional responses. Don't encourage them by giving them what they want.

Ignore them instead. Trolls lose *all* of their power if you don't give them any attention. I know it's difficult to let the troll have the last word, but you'll prove that you're the grown-up in the situation. If they continue to harass you, report them. If enough people report the troll, the site's moderators will take action and remove the troll. Until that time, you can mute the troll or block them from your page.

But why do people enjoy being trolls? Well, these are often people who suffer from low self-esteem. When online, insecure people can easily achieve some kind of power to hold without actually having to face others directly. Fear and anxiety are the building blocks of low self-esteem, and the Internet makes it really easy to vent those negative emotions through alter egos and fake accounts. Internet trolls live on the Internet 24/7, always ready to insult someone. If they manage to hurt or upset someone, they consider this a victory. But if you're living in your parents' basement at twenty-eight years of age and spend your time hating on everything and everyone on the Internet, who's the real loser?

And remember, kids: don't feed the trolls!

4. Revenge Porn

Maybe you've never heard about revenge porn, but if you know what revenge is, and you know what porn is, I'm sure you can put two and two together. Revenge porn is a type of online harassment. It happens when someone posts or distributes explicit photos or videos from their ex-partner without his or her permission. The pictures or videos end up all over forums, websites, their own social media, anonymous networks, and so on, and they usually include the victim's name and a mean caption.

Becoming the victim of revenge porn can do serious damage to a person's life: anyone who Googles their name, including future employers or lovers, will find the porn pictures. Other than jeopardize the victim's future career and love life, revenge porn can also destroy a person's self-esteem, body image, and their trust in others.

If it happens to you, the first thing to remember is that none of it is your fault. Revenge porn is abuse. Of course, there'll be people who tell you that you should've known better, and sure, thanks, Captain Hindsight, but what if you trusted the other person? What if you shared a lot of intimate information because the other person made you believe they were safe to do so with? What if you were in a relationship for a while and nothing in his behavior made you suspect he was capable of this type of harassment?

Unfortunately, online revenge porn is nothing new and has become an increasingly large problem over the past couple years. It's incredibly hard to put a stop to this revenge-porn epidemic, because smartphones (and other devices) with cameras that can record, edit, and share media in a matter of seconds are everywhere. As soon as a picture or video is leaked, there's no way to take it back. However, you can try to control the damage by making sure the offending picture or video is deleted right away.

Here are some quick, practical tips on how to prevent or deal with revenge porn:

1. First of all: prevention, prevention, prevention! Think long and hard before you trust someone with your private photos and videos. Before you take a leap of faith, remember that the other person might break your trust. Deep down, you *know* why you probably shouldn't be sending private photos to someone online, because any material you send might come back to bite you in the ass. Yes, apps like Snapchat and Cyberdust can guarantee that your pics will be deleted as soon as they are viewed. But they can't promise you that your recipient won't take a screenshot first! Talk about this with your partner so you can come to an agreement that matches your expectations and strengthens your trust before you share anything private and personal with them via social media or text.

2. Don't be sorry you took the pictures or video. You made the choice to create them, not to distribute them. So don't beat yourself up if you do end up being a victim of revenge porn. Victim blaming is never the right way to go. Besides, think of the many celebrities who have been the target of revenge porn. They are in the public eye and their photos spread a thousand times as fast. But do they let it stop them from sharing private footage with their loved ones? Of course not!

3. If you become the victim of revenge porn, try to stay calm. Don't make it worse by retaliating against the person who's behind it, because that's a perfect way to mess up things even more. Letting your emotions cloud your vision won't help the situation. Take a deep breath before you do *anything* else.

4. Take legal action if you feel you want to. You can find a list of legal resources on cybercivilrights.org. It's important to have many kinds of evidence against the person who uploaded sensitive content about you. If you want to use the privacy law, you have to prove that the person is harassing you. Take as many screenshots as possible, because the person can and will delete all the evidence sooner or later. Most states in the United States have anti-cyberbullying laws in place that (in some cases) might be applied to revenge porn. However, you'll still have to prove that the pornographic images or video were posted out of emotional distress or revenge. In order to have the porn itself removed, it might be best to play the copyright law card; this is a useful strategy if you are the one who made the pictures or videos and not the other person.

5. Manage your online search results. If you want to avoid future disasters in your professional or private life, be proactive and hide the content through good search engine optimization (SEO). Take control of your Google results by adding neutral and positive content, so people see that stuff first when they Google your name. If you surround your name with positive search results, this'll help minimize the negative impact of the revenge porn to your reputation.

6. Take time for yourself. Recovering from this kind of situation is not easy, and it won't be a smooth ride. It might be a while before you'll be able to trust people again, including yourself. I know being patient can be difficult, but as cliché as it might sound, time does heal all wounds and people will forget about the incident eventually. In the meantime, make sure to focus on you and take care of yourself.

Remember that you're not alone in this situation, even if it might feel that way. Talk to a friend or a relative about what happened to you and look for the emotional support you need. No matter how big of a mess you're in right now, you'll find a light at the end of the tunnel with the help of your friends and family!

5. Catfish

When I was in art school in 2010, my class had to watch a new documentary no one had heard about before. I groaned at the idea of having to sit through the whole thing, because I felt it had nothing to do with art and was probably going to be just another boring documentary about some artist who thought he'd created something new and extraordinary.

CATFISH

We started to watch the film, and it was about a guy who met a girl on the Internet, and they started dating online soon after. The guy was a really handsome young man, and the girl he was dating was equally gorgeous. Her name was Megan. From the moment they met online, they'd been chatting nonstop. They started calling each other on the phone and exchanging spicy sexts. So obviously, the two wanted to meet up in real life to see how things would work out. So the guy and a group of his filmmaking buddies set out to go meet her.

That's when the first red flag began popped. The filmmaker discovered that the musical covers Megan had been sending him were fake, but the team encouraged him to continue the relationship for the sake of the documentary. They wanted to know if Megan was really Megan.

After many months, the guy and Megan finally arranged to meet. When they arrive at her house, the filmmaker's fear was confirmed—the beautiful young girl he'd fallen for online turned out to be an older woman named Angela. Angela admitted that she'd created a Facebook page for Megan and had invented an entire community of family and friends around her to make it look more realistic. In the nine months the guy and Angela were chatting, they exchanged more than 1,500 messages.

If you haven't it figured it out already, the movie we watched in art class was Nev Schulman's *Catfish*. The film was a huge critical and commercial success and provided the inspiration for the enormously popular MTV show.

A catfish is someone who pretends to be someone else online, either for attention or to dupe or scam someone. The deception often involves love and emotions, which makes it harder to cope with. Catfishing stories hardly ever result in a real-life relationship because of all the lying that's been going on. A catfish will lie about anything and everything: his or her identity, gender, age, location, occupation, financial status, body type, and even his or her feelings.

HELP! I'VE BEEN CATFISHED!

The general rule is if someone seems too good to be true online, they probably are. If you notice that an online acquaintance's life is a little too perfect or unrealistic, it's not unlikely that you're talking to a person with a faked profile, created with pictures taken from online sources. Other signs that you might be dealing with a catfish include:

- The conversations are getting really serious really fast. Actually, too fast. A catfish will try to worm his way into your personal life ASAP, so he can pretend to care about you.
- The other person doesn't want to show her face. She'll claim that she doesn't have a smartphone, webcam, or Skype. Nowadays, a webcam is really not that expensive and not being able to download Skype is a just a flat-out lie. A lot of people have smartphones nowadays, too, which makes video-chatting even easier.
- He has an excuse for being broke and asks if you can send him a small amount of money to pay for something, like a plane ticket he needs to visit a sick relative. It always starts with something small he needs, but he'll then need more. Remember never to give away your bank account information to *anyone*, especially a stranger online.
- If you ask her to send a selfie or just a regular picture, she'll always have an excuse for not sending one right away. Of course, that's because she's likely not who she claims to be, and she needs time to look for a picture to steal from the person she's pretending to be.
- When you try to confront him about being fake, he always seem to have an excuse ready. He reassures you that he loves you and that you'll meet up soon. He talks you up and make you feel good. Don't buy into the bullshit, and try not to fall for his pretty words.
- Her life appears to be extremely hectic, and she seems to have a lot of problems concerning her family, love life, or financial situation. She'll try to deceive you with sob stories, so you'll feel sorry for her and be more willing to go along with anything she proposes.
- Something about the other person seems off, but you can't tell exactly what it is. If you have suspicions, you are probably right. Your gut feeling is telling you that something is terribly wrong and that you should end all contact with the person immediately.

WHAT TO DO ABOUT CATFISHING

First of all, you have to be sure you're being catfished. The catfish checklist above is just an indication, so try to make absolutely sure you're being deceived before you do anything.

Here are a few things you can do to avoid any further damage from a nasty online catfish:

1. **Stay calm.** Honestly, being catfished can be as painful as a breakup, and having your suspicions confirmed can be crushing. Ask the other person tricky questions: a catfish will not be able to give a plausible or bullshit-free answer.

2. **Report, block, and delete.** The damage between you two is already done, but you'll probably want to stop the catfish from targeting others. Report the catfish to the platform where the catfishing took place (a dating site, a social network). Dating websites usually have a reporting section where you can share your story and where the catfish can be blocked or banned.

3. **Never meet up with people you don't know or trust.** The catfish might pretend to be a boy or girl your age who's interested in a real-life relationship, when, in fact, they're an adult with other intentions. Always be careful when you arrange to meet someone you know only from the Internet. Read more online dating dos and don'ts earlier in this chapter.

4. **Do you want to stay in touch with your catfish?** This might seem like a crazy question, but in general there are two types of catfish: those who pretend to be someone else just to mess with you or scam you, and those who lie about who they are because they're too insecure to interact with you as themselves. I wouldn't really recommend staying in the touch with the first group, but you might stay friends with a catfish of the second type. It's not crazy to feel that way, either; you've shared so many moments together, and it is completely up to you to decide if you want to continue the relationship or not.

THE CATFISH AFTERMATH

Being catfished means having your feelings hurt by someone you trusted. You might have shared some intimate moments or romantic dreams for the future with that person that now are quashed. Whether you decide to stay friends (or even more) or not, the choice is up to you. However, you should allow yourself some time to process what happened and how you can protect yourself from a repeat down the road.

It's perfectly okay to feel angry with the person who deceived you, but remember you're not alone. Catfishing is a common phenomenon: there are thousands of people out there who've been tricked just like you have and who know exactly how you're feeling. The catfish is always wrong, so don't blame yourself for putting your faith in that person.

Don't let your emotions guide your actions. Before you do anything, take a deep breath and look at the damage. How bad is it? Did you share any private details, such as passwords or bank

information, with the person? If so, change all of those passwords ASAP and call your bank; they'll answer any questions you might have about scamming and fraud and can help you protect yourself and your money.

No matter how painful, being catfished can turn into a valuable life lesson. Treat it like you would any other breakup and try to take something meaningful from the experience. Where did it go wrong, according to you? Were there any red flags? If so, what were they? The more you learn from this, the sooner you'll be able to go on with your life. Everyone has their own way of coping with this kind of betrayal, but I promise you'll be more careful the next time you meet someone new online.

FOUR TIPS FOR A HEALTHY INFORMATION DIET

Clay Johnson is a blogger and the author of *The Information Diet: A Case for Conscious Consumption*. In his opinion, a healthy information diet is one that is limited to a couple hours spent online or engaging with media a day. His own personal diet consists of six hours a day in total. In those six hours, he does all kinds of digital activities that require his attention but that don't involve human interaction. If an activity involves a URL, a mouse, or a remote control, it has to take place within the six-hour time frame. He doesn't include accidental exposure, such as advertisements or music in grocery stores.

Of those six hours, he spends about two hours on entertainment and four hours on work-related research and communication. On weekends, he spends the full six hours on whatever he wants. The only condition is that he only gets six hours and not a minute more. By limiting his digital intake to six hours a day, he's forced to do other stuff, like go for a walk or cook a good dinner. He claims that this trick has been a hugely beneficial, not only to his productivity, but also to his marriage and his overall health.

Johnson also believes that, in the same way junk food leads to health problems, junk information kills our productivity and efficiency and makes us ignorant. On his blog, *InfoVegan*, he shares a bunch of tips for a healthy information diet. I collected some of his most important tips and added a few of my own:

Keep Track of Your Consumption

Time yourself and start monitoring what kind of information you're taking in. It's a bit like a food diet, where you keep track of what you eat every day, except you're examining your digital media intake instead of your calories. Get yourself a notebook and write down what you're taking in (such as movies, television, social media). When you're doing something on your computer or your smartphone, use a tool like rescuetime.com; it runs secretly in the background and keeps track of time spent on apps and websites. It'll give you a pretty accurate overview of how much time you spend on your devices and what you spend that time doing. In the beginning, you'll be surprised to learn just how much precious time you've wasted on useless apps such as Twitter and Facebook.

Create a Healthy Information Meal Plan

As with a normal meal, you can plan your information meals before-hand. Create a good mix between news (*New York Times*, Google News, Huffington Post . . . whatever reliable news source you choose), nonfiction (anything of your interest, *not* just stuff you look at for work or school), social networks (keep this part to a minimum, as social media is usually only useful to help you kill some time), and enrichment (a part of your daily consumption, and this part is often forgotten or neglected, and should consist of podcasts, TED talks, documentaries).

Set Up Your System

There are a number of handy desktop tools out there to help keep you productive and focused. Some of them are apps that work on your smartphone, which is a notorious attention-killer! Here's a short list of what you can do to help you stay more focused while online:

- **Adblock:** Seriously, get an ad blocker. It's a browser extension that blocks advertisements on major websites. It works for Google Chrome and Mozilla Firefox.
- **Facebook Notification Settings:** Uncheck the box next to "Send me important updates and summary e-mails instead of individual notification e-mail." Next, visit the notification settings on Facebook and uncheck every box. You can also choose to disable the ads in your Facebook timeline.
- **Twitter Settings:** Uncheck every box on the Twitter Settings page.
- **Put your phone on "do not disturb" mode:** On iPhones it's the little half-moon icon in your control center. If you're an Android user, you might want to check your phone's settings for available options. Now you won't be disturbed by any unnecessary notifications.
- **Forest:** This is a great app that my friends use when they are studying. Basically, you plant a tree whenever you want to focus. You choose for how long you want to leave your phone alone, and the tree will grow for the amount of time you selected. The tree dies if you leave the app. If you keep building your forest, every single tree represents a time span during which you were focused on something else (or at least not playing with your phone).

Put down your phone sometimes and focus on what's important in life!

Keep the Balance

Adapting to a new diet is always hard in the beginning, but being persistent pays off. Sooner or later you'll learn what's important enough to attract your attention and to hold it. Mindlessly scrolling

through Facebook, Instagram, and Twitter feeds are not going to help you fall asleep. Reading a book, writing a poem, or working out will. Of course, technology helps us a lot in our daily lives—at school and at work. Just remember to maintain a healthy balance between what's important and what's useless in the media you consume and you will feel more productive and focused on a daily basis.

TO POST OR NOT TO POST

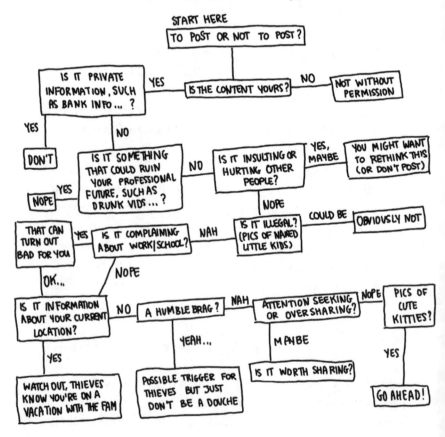

STAYING TRUE TO YOUR (VIRTUAL) SELF

Perhaps the real question to ask is, "Why do we fake being happy on social media and how do we stop ourselves from doing it?" This is one of the biggest questions I struggled with as a teen. My generation grew up with the rise of smartphones and social media apps. Whenever we post online, we're usually giving our network an update about our (private and professional) lives. It's basically the same thing as going for drinks with friends, but like, a whole lot of friends you don't really know in a huge, crowded club.

I think almost everyone feels a sense of being let down when our latest picture doesn't get as many likes as we'd hoped. How many of us have posted a selfie, desperately waiting for that one person to see it and he doesn't? How many of us have been jealous, at least once, of our friend's bikini pic from the beach last summer? Social media is a whole different world, where we say and post things we probably wouldn't say or do in real life. On social media, we can pretend to have whatever and be whoever the f*** we want.

We fake a lot of things online, and it's time to face the fact that it's kinda ridiculous. We compare ourselves to fake images and try to shush our insecurities by creating fake pictures ourselves. That's our way of telling our social media followers that our life is great, that we're doing fine, and that we're just great always! But who are we kidding, actually, other than ourselves? Here's some classic things we like to embellish on social media:

- **Our looks.** We know our best angles and the cutest filters, and that's how we can pretend to look almost perfect. But honestly, we don't look anything like ourselves anymore. We have become truly skilled in the art of faking the perfect selfie, and it usually takes a lot—finding the right lighting that makes our features pop, looking for the perfect angle, and holding a weird pose that is kinda breaking our backs. Yup, fifty likes guaranteed!

THINGS YOU DON'T SEE ON SOCIAL MEDIA BUT ARE SUPER NORMAL :

— ME, BEING STRESSED OUT BY THE TINIEST THING

ME, LOOKING — AT MY BEST, CHILLING AND ENJOYNING LIFE TO THE FULLEST

THINGS YOU DO SEE ON SOCIALS BUT DON'T HAPPEN EVERYDAY :

• **Our relationships.** You know, all the cutie patootie pics of couples on vacation? Or their anniversary celebration? Or their picnic together? Or their canoe trip? We all know that *one* couple that just has to post everything on social media, hashtagging #couplegoals #forever. I bet they are fighting every day but feel the need to make sure everyone thinks their relationship is all that.

- **Partying and going to concerts.** Let's be honest, how many videos of friends attending a concert or festival have you actually watched? Most of them are poor quality and just plain deafening. The reason why our friends post them is to make sure that everyone knows they were at the concert or party. The content doesn't matter in the least.
- **Food.** I hardly ever take any food pics, because I've usually finished half my dish by the time I remember to take a picture. Unless taking pictures of food is your job, no one really cares about your #foodporn Instagram pic. First of all: the viewers can't taste it, so that's a bummer. And second: it probably doesn't look half as good in the pictures as it does in real life.
- **Traveling.** Astonishing sunsets, beautiful local markets, beaches, and mountains. We've seen it all in your stories. But where are the delayed-flight selfies? The picture of you putting on aloe vera after being severely sunburned? Or that time you got food poisoning? I'm kidding about the last one (am I?), but instead of showing the reality of traveling, we prefer the picture-perfect moment on the Golden Gate Bridge in the golden hour, with an amazeballs filter to top it off.
- **Our attitude.** We pretend to be a lot cooler, more assertive, and confident than we really are. To be honest, it's pretty easy to create an online persona that has almost zero in common with the person you really are. Our lives are messy, and we all suffer setbacks and ride emotional roller coasters. But at all costs, we'll stay cool on our social network sites.

I have to admit, I'm guilty of all this, too. So for the sake of everyone, myself included, we should give some serious thought to how we can change the way we present ourselves on social media. Our obsession with flaunting our lives is both the cause and the effect of the brag culture we've created and are now stuck in. Social media tends to be some kind of popularity contest. (Who has the most likes? Who has the best pics? Who has the best body?) Whether we mean to or not, whether we like it or not, we all judge others by their online presence and are judged by them in return.

But there's hope! So many people on social media are absolutely *not* what they claim to be. They seem to have a lot of friends, awesome dinners, and the best parties, but does that mean they're necessarily happier than us? Probably not, and that's exactly why you shouldn't believe everything you see on your social media feed. Don't attach too much value or meaning to it, and don't compare yourself to everything you see while scrolling. Everyone, literally everyone, has their bad moments or days.

Social media is not real life, but we already knew that. The tricky part is this: although we all know that social media is one big charade, we still keep taking those pics and posting those statuses. Why is that? Because social media is everywhere, and thus we live in a world where oversharing has become the norm. At the same time, we live in a society that seems to think beauty is more important than skills. And sadly, we get most of our self-esteem from the confirmation of our friends and peers nowadays instead of finding it within ourselves.

We like to think we're super social and connected, but in reality, we are lonelier than ever. Damn, what can we actually do to turn this around?

Now that you understand how it happens and, most important, why it happens, you can try to tackle the problem at its roots. If you don't want to give up social media (yet), that's perfectly fine. I'm the last person to tell you you should. But you might want to consider trying the following:

- **Live consciously.** Be aware of the fact that you automatically grab your phone when your date gets up to go to the bathroom. Why do you do that? Because you feel awkward just sitting there by yourself, and you don't know what to do with your hands. Look around! Pay more attention to the things that are happening around you.
- **Put your phone away when you're having dinner.** Next time you visit a restaurant, play the phone stacking game: everyone who is at the dinner has to put her phone down on the table, on top of everybody else's phones, creating a tall stack. The first person to touch her phone has to pay the bill.

- **Ditch the perfectionism.** Do you generally walk down the street with a filter over your eyes? No, and neither do I. Don't waste your time creating the perfect picture that doesn't even look like the real you. You're only fooling yourself.
- **Build more genuine and face-to-face relationships.** Try leaving your phone at home for one full day. You'll be so much more aware of your surroundings. Smile, greet people you pass on the street. Connect with people in real life.

Remember that self-esteem comes from the inside, not from the approval of others with a simple like or love button.

THE IMPORTANCE OF YOUR ONLINE PRIVACY

Let's say you're walking home from school, and you suddenly notice you're being followed by someone you don't know. They follow you all the way back to your house. Creepy, right? And great, now they know where you live. How does that make you feel?

Scared? You have every right to be terrified.

What if I told you it's really not that difficult at all to find out where people live, even if they've never explicitly shared that information, and even without physically stalking them? Do the test yourself: go online and time how long it takes you to find out some pretty personal information about someone you don't know at all. If you do a little bit of digging, I bet you can at least find that person's gender, age, home country, current location, profession, marital situation, pets, children, and so on. People usually aren't very protective of this kind of private information. When asked why they give so many details about their life away on social media, their answer is often that they have nothing to hide or be embarrassed about. That might be the case, but they're missing the point. Being careless about the information you share online can be dangerous.

Why is it so dangerous, you might wonder? Because our private information is *so* precious. On the Internet, data is invaluable. Information is power and money. People will steal, sell, and analyze any information they can get their hands on. Websites and apps keep track of every move you make, and gathering data is a big part of what websites are designed to do. By data I mean, who we are and what we do online. We leave a digital trail every time we shop online, book a vacation, or even when we're chatting with our friends! The more we do any of those things, the more information about us is registered and logged.

Okay, you might think, but why is privacy so important?

We all have stuff that we don't want other people to know. And that's fine! For example, you wouldn't want the whole world to know how much you earn or how well you do at school. You might not want your medical records and certainly not your bank account information accessible to just anyone. And what about your menstrual cycle? Some things you simply want to keep to yourself, and that's why we have to protect our right to privacy both in person and online.

Companies track and use whatever information they can find about you. I once purchased a kitten collar, and before I knew it, other companies started e-mailing me about their cat products, and all the advertisements I saw on YouTube suddenly were for cat food. Based on what sites had learned about me (how old my kitten was, my previous cat-related purchases) companies smacked me around the ears with other cat stuff. Which is super creepy, if you really think about it.

No matter how easy it is to get used to all of this, it is not *normal*. You should remember that this kind of information is, and always will be, yours. Companies will try to steal data on you to better market their product. So as much as you can, protect what is yours.

I collected some useful tips to help you protect your online privacy, inspired by the blog of a famous Internet security service called Norton:

- **Secure your passwords.** Make your passwords as difficult as you possibly can. Make them difficult to guess, make them nonsensical, and use lots of symbols and numbers. Also: change your passwords regularly, as they becomes easy to track after a while.
- **Check your privacy settings.** Who can see your content?
- **Remember that everything you've once posted somehow stays on the Internet:** That's called a digital footprint.
- **Be careful with free Wi-Fi hotspots.** They're not always secure, and you don't even know what kind of information you're sharing with this public wifi. Never handle stuff that involves sensitive information, such as bank transactions, on public Wi-Fi networks.
- **Delete any data that you no longer use.** If you haven't used an app or program in a long time, just delete it.
- **Never post your phone number or home address anywhere online.** Be careful who you share this information with.

Chapter Nine

SOCIETY VS. ME

I am part of society. You are, too. We all are. But what kind of society do you want to live in? Since we are all part of it, we do have something to say about it, don't we?

My grandpa is always saying things like, "When I was your age, things were better." Does this sound familiar to you? People (mostly grown-ups and the elderly) say this to express their frustration with "kids these days" (a.k.a. the younger generation). The other day, however, I caught myself uttering the same exact sentence when I saw a young boy riding a hoverboard down the street while playing with a fidget spinner in his hand. I genuinely thought it was danger-ous to spin and drive at the same time, so I mentally labeled this kid somehow dumber than I was at his age. Maybe I'm acting just as old as my grandpa?

I thought the same thing when I overheard a young girl crying and screaming in a toy store. She was yelling and calling her mom names, which made me think about my own childhood. Was I that rude as a child? Was I that spoiled when I was younger? After asking myself those questions, I could suddenly relate to older adults; it kinda

"GRANDMA, TELL ME ABOUT THE TIME WHEN YOU WERE YOUNG!"

– WELL, BACK IN MY DAYS, KIDS WERE DRIVING ELECTRIC VEHICLES WITH FIDGET SPINNERS ON THEIR HEADS.

THOSE WERE THE DAYS.

makes sense for them to think that what the kids are doing is weird or not as good as before.

Every generation has its doubts about the one to follow, and this has been going on for many generations. English satirist Douglas Adams says: "Anything that is in the world when you're born is normal and ordinary and is just a natural part of the way the world works. Anything that's invented between when you're fifteen and thirty-five is new and exciting and revolutionary and you probably can get a career in it. Anything invented after you're thirty-five is against the natural order of things."

So, naturally, our parents and grandparents aren't familiar with everything new our generation grows up with. The last few decades have been a roller-coaster ride of digital revolutions and the growth of social media. Our parents might understand this new world (to a certain extent), since they experienced the rise of the first personal computers and the early Internet era. Maybe they even helped shape the new technological landscape. This evolution, however, is logically more difficult for our grandparents to wrap their heads around as they never knew a world as digital as the one we live in today.

What's the best way to close this generational gap? Our (grand) parents should be more open to our culture and immerse themselves in it. If our parents and teachers would simply try to get involved in a positive way by talking to us and asking questions about video games, music, videos, trends, and the like, that would be a tiny step forward. All the new Internet gadgets and apps make our parents slightly uncomfortable because they are unfamiliar. Believe me when I tell you they simply can't help their ignorance; they don't know as much about social media as we do. Whenever they need your help with setting up a Facebook or Instagram account, try not to get annoyed, but see it as an opportunity for you to help your parents better understand the world we take for granted. The more they "get" the things that are important in your life, the better for you!

If we want to close the generation gap between us and our parents and grandparents, we'll have to help each other out. They can help us, too, by teaching us some common sense about assimilating new media and modern content into their lives, and we can help them whenever they have difficulty understanding new digital stuff.

And maybe, just maybe, I'll bring a fidget spinner along the next time I go cruising on my hoverboard. Maybe I don't know what I'm missing.

CHANGING THE WORLD: EVERYONE CAN DO IT

When I was kid, I believed that every grown-up was capable of changing the world. As I grew up, I slowly became discouraged by the way our world actually works, and I soon realized that changing the world was not going to be as easy as I once thought it would. I truly

CHANGE THE WORLD - BUCKETLIST

☐ ADOPT A PET FROM A SHELTER

☐ SHARE A MEAL WITH A HOMELESS PERSON

☐ BE VEGETARIAN FOR ONE DAY A WEEK

☐ SAY "PLEASE" AND "THANK YOU" EVERYTIME

☐ SUPPORT SOMEONE ELSE'S DREAM

☐ WRITE A LETTER TO SOMEONE YOU HAVEN'T SEEN IN A WHILE

☐ DON'T TAKE YOURSELF TOO SERIOUSLY

☐ DO A RANDOM ACT OF KINDNESS

☐ PICK UP SOME TRASH

☐ DO SOME VOLUNTEER WORK

☐ INVEST IN A LOCAL BUSINESS

☐ SAY "HELLO"

☐ FORGIVE

☐ GIVE UP YOUR SEAT

☐ BE FRIENDLY TO THE WAITER/WAITRESS

☐ DON'T ANSWER HATE WITH HATE

☐ SMILE MORE

☐ COMPLAIN LESS

☐ BE MORE GRATEFUL

☐ BE YOURSELF!!!

☐ STAND UP FOR SOMEONE

☐ HELP SOMEONE WITH THEIR HOMEWORK

☐ DONATE BLOOD

☐ PLANT A GARDEN

☐ BUY FAIRTRADE FOOD

believed I could singlehandedly end poverty worldwide and put a stop to wars and save all the animals and achieve world peace when I was a little kid. Like many other people out there, I wanted to make big changes so the world would be a better place for all of us.

As I got older, though, it become clear that it was impossible for me to achieve any of those things on my own. But big changes aren't always about big actions. Big changes are usually the result of doing little things, but doing them consistently. And that's a comforting thought, knowing that we all *can* make a difference, even if it's small. It's even more comforting to learn that every change starts from within yourself: by making small adjustments to our own lives, and encouraging our friends and family to do the same, we can create a snowball effect. The key is to be consistent.

HOW TO EXPRESS YOURSELF WITHOUT BEING RUDE ABOUT IT

Being able to express your opinion is your personal right. However, being rude about it is not. We all have our own beliefs, values, and perspectives. At some point in our lives, we will encounter people who don't agree with us. But even when we're not on the same page, we should always tolerate and respect other people's opinions. During my teenage years, that was something I struggled with a lot because 1) I was afraid to express my own opinion when I disagreed with someone, and 2) I was scared of other people's reactions if our opinons differed. Other people's feelings were more important to me than my own.

Learning how to communicate in a nonviolent way has helped me dismantle quite a few personal, professional, and political differences.

First of all, listen to what the other person is saying before you answer. It is very impolite and disrespectful to interrupt someone, and you can't expect the other person to be respectful if you aren't. Use the phrases "in my view," "in my opinion," "I feel," "I think," "if you ask me," "to be honest, I am convinced that," "by this I mean," "to be more precise, I would appreciate if," and so on. Don't use phrases such as, "you're wrong, let me tell you why I am right," "loser, you don't know what you're talking about," "you always do this or that," "don't be so sensitive," etc.

When you're having an argument with someone who's your friend or partner, it can be difficult not to let it get personal. Still, you should try to avoid launching personal attacks, as they add no value to the conversation; they only bring the other person down. Remember that your goal is to present your own ideas, not to undermine someone else's. You don't have to agree with what the other person is saying, but trying to see things from their point of view is a good step toward understanding each other a little better.

If there's an actual problem between you and your friend, family member, or partner, and you're not just having a debate about politics or whatever, remember that there are two sides to every argument. It's a mistake to only consider your own. You don't have to agree with them if you have a different opinion, but don't attribute your emotions to other people.

THE ART OF BEING A FEMINIST

The word *feminist* has gained a negative connotation in recent years, but it has been widely misinterpreted throughout history. A feminist is someone who believes in the social, political, and economic equality of the sexes. A feminist is not someone who hates men. A feminist is not a woman who can't find a man. A feminist is also not someone who hates anything remotely girly or feminine. It's time to take the word back to its true meaning.

Novelist and feminist Chimamanda Ngozi Adichie wrote the book *We Should All Be Feminists*, based on the TEDx Talk she gave in 2013. Adichie's defines a feminist as "a man or a woman who says: 'Yes, there's a problem with gender as it is today, and we must fix it. We must do better.'" And that's a definition I can relate to and identify with. Some people believe feminism means that women should have the right to choose the lifestyle they want; others think it means men and women should be equal in all aspects. Neither interpretation is wrong, but how you choose to understand the concept of feminism is completely up to you.

Basically, everyone can be a feminist. That holds true as long as you support the general idea that men and women should be treated equally. What about the biological differences between men and women? We can't ignore them, right? Certainly, there are biological differences between men and women. We have different biological abilities. We have different hormones and different sexual organs. But we're all human beings, and one gender is not superior to the other.

Back in the day—and we're talking hundreds of thousands of years ago—the person who had the most muscle was likely to be the leader of the group, and in most cases, that person was a man. But nowadays, we no longer need superior physical strength to go hunting or to survive in the wilderness, so whoever we put in charge these days is not necessarily the strongest dude in the group. Nowadays, we need someone who is creative, intelligent, innovative . . . and there's no gender linked to any of those key attributes.

In her TEDx Talk, Adichie promoted raising girls and boys equally. She openly asked, "What if boys and girls were raised not to link masculinity with money? What if the attitude wasn't 'the boy has to pay,' but rather 'whoever has more money should pay?'"

If it were that easy, I'd wake up in the morning and throw on on whatever the f*** I wanted, without having to worry about getting catcalled on the streets. If it were that easy, I wouldn't have to deal with sexist jokes about my Thai heritage. If it were that easy, other girls and women would've supported me more often, instead of seeing me as a competitor and putting me down.

Feminism is not about how you look or what you wear. It's not about who you date or fall in love with. It's not about thinking you deserve more than someone else. It's about thinking you deserve the same. Women are already strong; we just want society to perceive us as strong, too.

Men are affected by gender-role expectations, as well, which tell them how to dress or act in given circumstances. Feminists believe that each individual, with her or his own unique set of strengths and talents, should be seen as a human being in her or his own right, not as a female or a male. According to the culture we live in, men are not supposed to cry or show emotions. And they are supposed to l ook masculine. They are expected to be career-obsessed go-getters who love beer and sports. So it's important to understand that the basic principle promoted in feminism does not only serve women— feminism strives to put an end to gender roles that impact both women *and* men.

THE SALARY GAP: MORE THAN JUST SOME DOLLARS

The salary gap, also known as the gender pay gap, is the difference between the salaries men and women make. The American Association of University Women (AAUW) recently released a report on the subject, titled "The Simple Truth about the Gender Pay Gap." The report exposes the mechanism behind the pay gap and how it affects women of all ages, races, and educational backgrounds. It also explains what we can do to close the gap.

In 2015, studies revealed that women working full-time in the US were typically paid only 80 percent of what men working the same jobs earned. Hello, 20-percent gap?! Since the 1970s, the salary gap has been steadily shrinking because more and more women received an education and entered the work force at a higher level. At the same time, men's wages have risen more slowly. However, the gap is unlikely to go away on its own. If the rate of change between 1960 and 2015 is any indication, women won't be paid the same salary as men until 2059.

Say what?

The salary gap affects all kinds of women. However, the gender gap is even larger for women of color: among full-time workers in 2015, Hispanic and Latina, African American, American Indian, Native Hawaiian, and other native women had lower annual incomes than non-Hispanic white and Asian American women. And as women grow older, their incomes tend to increase with age, but that increase slows down at age forty-five and tends to decrease after fifty-five. Generally, at age thirty-five, women earn around 90 percent of what men working the same job are paid.

At first glance, getting a good education seems like a foolproof solution to earning equal pay, right? Well, while it has proven to be a useful tool for increasing women's earnings, it's still not enough to close the gender wage gap. Why? Because no matter the level of academic achievement, women still earn less than men, just because they are *women*. In some cases, the pay gap *increases* along with the level of education. The infuriating conclusion: a woman can get a top-notch education, but her salary will still be determined by her sex and her race.

THE PAY GAP

If all of this is a bit too abstract, here's a couple of examples (the numbers are from 2015):

- Female truck drivers usually get paid $632 a week, while their male coworkers receive $751 for doing the *exact* same job.
- Female software developers typically earn $1,415 weekly, while male software developers make $1,751 in the same week.
- Female financial managers are paid $1,130 per paycheck, whereas their male counterparts get paid $1,732. That's a gap of 35 percent!

This isn't right, but you *can* do something about it!

Women can adopt strategies to negotiate equal pay. The AAUW organizes workshops to empower women, encouraging them to stand up for themselves when it comes to salary, benefits, and promotions. The workshop has taught many women valuable skills that will be useful for years to come. Check out their website (salary.aauw.org) to discover free workshops hosted in your area. Can't find a workshop in your neighborhood? Organize your own, or inspire your school to host one. The workshops are meant for students and professionals alike, so you can take your mom, sister, or friend with you!

Find out if equal pay laws are strong in your state, and if not, write to your Congress person to move their asses on equal pay!

Struggling with the Idea of Being a Feminist

Society has come a long way in the past century, and if it wasn't for all the feminists who opened their mouths and took to the streets to fight for what was rightfully theirs, women wouldn't be able to vote today. But even in 2017, the world still needs feminism. For both women and men. We'll need feminism until everyone is free to get married to the person she loves; until a number of countries abolish female circumcision practices that are mutilating their baby girls and women; until certain cultures stop seeing women as possessions to be bought and sold; and until men and women who work the same job are paid the same salary. Until all of those things (and *many* more) are fixed, yes, we'll need feminists.

Feminism has helped me accept myself more, and it's made me realize that I can wear what I want to wear, behave how I want to behave, and be who I am, no matter what other people might think. I love wearing my three-piece suit, and I don't care if it looks "masculine" to some. I think I look bomb in it. The general message here is that equality is key, even in the politically turbulent times we live in.

So *should* you be a feminist? Maybe you already are without even knowing it. Or maybe you're not and don't want to be labeled as one. That's okay. Some people don't feel the need to express their opinion about this topic, and that's perfectly fine. But it is interesting to learn about sexism in our society and what people are doing to fight it.

I consider myself a feminist, and for me, that label goes beyond equal rights. Feminism is about accepting and tolerating both genders and everything in between. I firmly believe that everyone should be able to make free choices in her life, and until we reach that point, I will continue to spread that message.

DISCRIMINATION: THE INS AND OUTS

When someone is discriminated against, it means people treat that person unfairly because of who they are or because of certain characteristics they possess. If you've ever been treated badly by another person just because you are (or you look) a little different, you've been the victim of discrimination. People can be discriminated against for the following:

- Your age
- Your gender
- Your race or ethnicity
- Your disabilities or handicaps
- Your religions and beliefs
- Pregnancy and maternity
- Your sexual preference and orientation
- Marriage and civil partnership

Chapter Nine: Society vs. Me

If you like to know more about these types, continue reading:

Age-related discrimination is called *ageism*, and you might have experienced this yourself at some point. It happens when a person is treated unfairly because of her age. Teenagers and senior citizens are typical victims of this type of discrimination. It seems that society has a way of considering younger and older peoples' voices and opinions as inferior. And that's not cool. Just because you're young doesn't mean you can't contribute to society or have great ideas or make sensible decisions. So never let anyone (not your teachers, peers, or community members) tell you you're not worth listening to.

Sadly, *racism* (particularly at school) is a lot more common than you might think. Racism entails the discrimination of a person on the basis of her skin color and can be seen as the failure of our society as a whole to provide a safe environment for people who have a different skin color, culture, or ethnicity.

If someone mistreats you because of your sex, gender, or perceived gender, you're a victim of *sexism*. Equal gender rights between men and women are still not a reality in society today, and we have a long way to go before the existing unbalance is corrected. All women (and men) should be able to express themselves freely, have access to birth control, have the right to choose abortion or adoption, be paid equally for the same job, and live free from (sexual) assault. This should go without saying, but clearly, it still doesn't. Until we get there, people will keep suffering from sexism.

Another type of discrimination is *homophobia*, which means you're treated badly because of your sexual orientation. Whether you are gay, lesbian, bisexual, transgender, two-spirit, or pansexual, *no one* has the right to harass you because of your sexual identity—ever. Some people are convinced that being gay (or anything else that isn't heterosexual) is wrong. The opposite is true, because no one has the right to discriminate or attack someone for being gay. Everyone, including every member of the LGBTQIA+ community, has the right to be attracted to whoever they want. No one should *ever* be judged or mistreated for being who they are, and that includes any sexual preference.

As a teenager, there were times when I was guilty of homophobia, too, albeit subconsciously and indirectly. For example, I used to say, "OMG, that's so gay" to describe something that I thought wasn't cool or funny. I was fourteen or so, and I honestly had no clue that I might've been hurting others with this homophobic phrase until one of my best friends, who *is* gay, explained how incredibly hurtful and disrespectful it was. I stopped using it then and there. This experience made me learn my lesson and ever since, I've been more aware of the power of words and how miserable they can make other people feel.

Transphobia is defined as the irrational fear or hatred of transgender people, or anyone who doesn't fit in with traditional male-female gender norms. It's important to note that there is a difference between "sex" and "gender": your sex is what you're born with between your legs (a vagina, a penis, or both). Your gender is whatever you choose to be—it comes from the inside and represents how you identify yourself. For some people, their sex and gender match; whereas for others, they don't. A transgender person can also self-identify as both genders at the same time or as neither of them. Sadly, transgender people often have to deal with transphobia in the form of verbal harassment or violence inflicted upon them by individual people. However, we should all be able to choose whoever we want to be and feel supported and accepted no matter how we self-identify.

When you're being treated badly because of a disability of any kind, you're a victim of *ableism*. It means that people wrongly judge you because of your disabilities. Ableism also means that you don't get the chances you deserve in your academic, professional, or personal life.

Discrimination can also happen against someone whose body type differs from the generalized norm or accepted standard. If someone is mistreated for having a larger body size, that's called *fat phobia*. The opposite, an irrational fear of skinny people, is called *macilentophobia*. We all know high school can be really horrible, especially if you're struggling with how you look. The media and society keep dictating what the ideal body looks like, but often that's an image that's nowhere near realistic to achieve. If someone doesn't fit the image, however, it can make them feel really terrible about themselves and they can develop a negative body image as a result. Our world needs to realize ASAP that health and beauty come in all shapes, colors, and sizes!

Classism happens when someone is treated unfairly because of her social status. Society tends to label people who have less money as less smart or interesting. However, having a certain amount of cash doesn't make you cool; it's your attitude toward other people and how you treat them that makes you cool and awesome. Having less money doesn't make you any less smart, desirable, or capable. If you're lucky enough to be able to buy whatever you want, you shouldn't feel guilty about it, but you should be aware of how privileged you are and understand that not everyone is as fortunate as you. If we support each other and overcome our struggles together, we become stronger and more successful in life. Other people might have to struggle a bit more than we do in order to succeed, but we can all help them out by breaking the stigma that surrounds the less fortunate.

These are some of the types of discrimination we might experience in our society. If you or someone you know is a victim of discrimination, there are a few things you can do to stop the injustice. Remember that it's never your fault and you're not alone in fighting this. Talk about the discrimination you are experiencing with an adult you trust and look for possible solutions. Discrimination is a phenomenon as old as time, and it's notoriously difficult to get rid of. There's no cure that can make discrimination disappear overnight. But we can look at ourselves and think about what we can do to help fight discrimination in our schools and lives. Here are a few ways you can help combat discrimination in your school, at home, or out in the community:

• Don't make offensive jokes. If someone makes one, calmly and politely tell them it's inappropriate, rude, and ignorant. Don't just remain silent on the issue.

• Think about the language you use and be careful with what you say. "That's so gay" or "That's retarded" are offensive and should never be said. If you find a phrase like that slipping out, own up to it, apologize, and try not to do it again.

- Ask questions and listen to others before you judge people.
- Learn about other cultures and differences: travel to countries you've never been before and get to know locals. Stay open minded when trying something new in another country or when you're with a family that has other values than you.
- Educate yourself and understand what is happening politically around the world. Don't just repeat what you've read but develop your own opinion about what's happening.
- Never accept anything homophobic, sexist, or racist. Stand up for someone who gets bullied on the train, at school, at work, or in public.

There are many forms of discrimination, but what they all have in common is the oppression of people. Discrimination takes power away from an individual or a group. People who are discriminated against can experience harassment, bullying, or mistreatment. If you're being abused at school, that's never your fault and you should always report it to a staff member, because school is supposed to make you feel safe.

We're all different, and that's what makes our world colorful and exciting. Bashing someone for being different than you is completely wrong. You wouldn't want others to mistreat *you*, right? If we can all learn to be a little more tolerant every day, society would be less of a hard world to live in for everyone who differs from "the norm."

FITTING IN AND FEELING LEFT OUT

Whether we are part of the popular crowd or are more of a floater, at some point, we all feel a bit left out and like we don't fit in.

In our hypersocial world, we are more likely to feel lonely and isolated than previous generations. We feel the need to be online constantly and to let the world know we exist, preferably by sharing gorgeous pictures and interesting status updates. That's just the online world, but even there you'll sometimes feel like you don't really fit in if you're being your true self.

At school, if you feel like you are the "weird one," it can come to a point where you don't feel comfortable in any group of friends, or where you feel more comfortable being on your own, even if you don't want to be. And that sucks. Feeling like you don't belong somewhere can make you feel lonely, sad, and depressed. Here's a number of possible reasons why you might feel as if you don't fit in, and what you can do about it:

• You don't think people at school will actually understand you. You feel like a complete stranger to everyone, and you simply haven't found any people who share the same interests as you yet. If you're a book lover, join a book club! Or maybe you're good at sports? Joining a school sports team can help you making a bunch of new friends. Sharing the same interests or hobbies is a great tool for starting a conversation.

• You are shy and constantly afraid of what people think of you. Being shy is okay—it's a part of who you are. Practice being more open and engaging. Give yourself and others a chance. People who accept you for who you are without criticizing you are truly "your people." Learn more about comfort zones and how to step out of them in chapter 1. Stepping out of your comfort zone and trying new things will help you open up more and expand your boundaries.

- You haven't completely embraced who you are yet. If you feel like you don't have any deep or profound friendships, but mostly shallow and superficial connections, you might want to find your inner self first. Figure out for yourself what you like, what your interests are, and what you're into. I used to like stuff that other kids in my class liked in order to fit in. But the truth is, finding what out what *you* like is way more pleasant! For example, I grew up with hard rock music. That music genre was never really popular with the children in my class. They liked pop music (which is totally okay), but I never felt that anyone gave my music a chance. Until one day, I gave a presentation about Black Sabbath in tenth grade. I was super nervous because I thought the girls would give me a stinky look, but at the end . . . it felt so awesome! I distinguished myself from the rest, and at the end of the presentation a girl came up to me and said it was a cool subject. We later became good (music) friends. Finding and accepting your typical self is the best building block for creating fulfilling friendships.

- Your BFF is not your BFF anymore. If you feel like you're slowly drifting apart, or the friendship just isn't working anymore, it might be because one (or both) of you has changed. Sometimes, the best policy is to let them go.

- You feel judged by people all the time. The best solution to this is to stop caring about what other people think and start enjoying yourself and your hobbies instead. Easier said than done? Yes. But will you feel better after you cut off toxic people? Absolutely. The trick is to be completely honest with yourself. Do you like these people anyway? Do you really value their opinions and why? Asking yourself these questions will help you with finding out if you hang around with these people for the wrong reasons. If you realize that some people around you aren't very supportive or uplifting, it's best to put yourself first and take action. Tell them frankly how you feel. This can go in two ways: they are willing to change something and be more accepting, or nothing changes and you both go your own way. Either way it's a win-win!

• People might make the mistake of thinking you *are* different, because you *look* different. Honestly, how many times have we misjudged people because of how they look? How many girls have turned out to be actually pretty cool and chill, despite their reputation and appearance? How many friends did we mislabel as weirdos before we actually got to know them? Exactly. I once received the tip to surprise others in a positive way. Say "hi" yourself for once. Go sit next to someone you've never met before. Have lunch with someone you think is cool but never dared to say something to. People often misjudge others. To erase this behavior, we can start being more open ourselves.

The most important thing to remember is that there's *nothing* wrong with you. Fitting in just takes a little courage and motivation sometimes, and the willingness to let go of the wrong people in your life so you can find the people you truly jive with.

FAMOUS PEOPLE: THE HAPPIEST PEOPLE IN THE WORLD . . . OR NOT?

My childhood dream was to become famous. I'm not kidding you. I always believed that famous people lived crazy, awesome lives (and that they all had swimming pools). I genuinely believed (and still believe?) that celebrities live a more privileged life.

I don't know what it was about being famous that appealed to me, specifically, but I just knew that's what I wanted to be. Fortunately, I kind of lost that dream as I got a little older. When I first started drawing Chrostin, I never thought of it as *the* way to success, because I never expected that people were actually going to like my work. Now I believe that I have other goals to reach with my webcomics. I want them to entertain, motivate, and inspire people. Yes, I *just* said that. I aspire to be an inspiration—not just for myself, but also for others. I want to encourage people to do whatever they want, to aim high and shoot for the stars. Because that's what I did, *too*. That's why I'm sitting here at 4:00 a.m. (don't judge me) writing this very paragraph of this book that I'm about to publish. Am I going to be famous for it? Probably not. But you can't say I never tried to leave my mark.

Back to real celebrities. I used to look up to people who accomplished a lot in their lives and worked their asses off to become what they always wanted to be. So in that sense, yes, I want the same. But I also ask myself if it's worth it. Are celebrities actually happy? Since I don't know any really famous people, I can't ask them. But I did some research and I found others who *did* get the chance to ask a number of famous people the million-dollar question: is fame, wealth, and material success the key to happiness?

There's plenty of celebrities who've talked openly about what success really does to them, and honestly? Their answers are really disappointing. As I kind of expected, but somehow didn't want to admit, famous people generally aren't happy, precisely *because* they are famous. Being famous, it turns out, isn't very fulfilling at all. In fact, some actors and musicians have even stated that, as their success grew larger and larger, so did their feelings of anxiety and depression.

Eric Clapton, a very famous rock star, admitted in interviews that despite having more than he could've ever imagined—an amazing career as a guitar god, cars, a beautiful house, a very bright future—he felt suicidal on a daily basis. Model Cara Delevingne once confirmed that, while we might think that owning beautiful things and feeling loved by everyone will make us truly happy, this isn't always the case. Lady Gaga once stated that she doesn't want to spend her days shaking hands and taking selfies, because it feels like a shallow thing to do when she has a lot more to offer than her image alone.

I soon understood that my obsession with fame was not based

on anything substantial; it was more of a hypothetical daydream. It's natural for us to think that celebrities have perfect lives, because that's how they're portrayed in the media (as the prettiest, wealthiest, coolest peeps on the planet). But listening to their behind-the-scenes stories, I now understand that they're just human beings. Like you and me. Except more famous.

To sum up, I still think it's okay to daydream about becoming a celebrity (because why not?). Just try to take the whole concept with a pinch of salt, and remember that there's so much more to life than being famous. And that fame doesn't necessarily mean happiness.

ON BEING A HAPPY PERSON

Model Cara Delevingne has stressed the importance of finding your true self and that your journey toward self-discovery is the most important one you'll ever make. Tupac, songwriter and rapper, once said that you should be able to look in the mirror and see your soul—that you should be able to look yourself in the eye and know that you didn't sell your soul. Bottom line: what's more important than being admired by the public is being valued and loved by the people who surround us and who make us feel alive. That is one way to become a happy person.

Tom Shadyac, comedian and producer, made me see that "our culture is obsessed with competition, where the winner gets it all. We should realize that we live in a culture where authenticity and creativity gets depressed and that's the reason why we are pitting against each other."

We blame society, but we are society.

So how can you be happy in a society where the best is only good enough?

HAPPINESS CHANGE LIST
LITTLE THINGS THAT IMPROVE YOUR HAPPINESS

O WRITE A LETTER TO YOUR (YOUNGER) SELF: OPEN NEXT YEAR

O BUY FLOWERS (FOR SOMEONE)

O DIGITAL DETOX

O CUT OUT ALL THE TOXIC PEOPLE IN YOUR LIFE

O LEARN HOW TO MEDITATE

O GO TO THE LIBRARY AND CHOOSE A RANDOM BOOK

O START A VISIONAL DIARY (WITH DRAWINGS, PHOTOS....)

O WRITE DOWN YOUR LIFE STORY

O DONATE CLOTHES YOU NO LONGER WEAR

O LEARN A TRICK AND SHOW IT TO EVERYONE

O STOP COMPARING YOURSELF TO OTHERS

O ORGANISE A PICNIC

O GO TO A MOTIVATIONAL EVENT (SUCH AS TEDxTALK)

O TRY TO BREAK A GUINESS WORLD RECORD

O DANCE LIKE NO ONE'S WATCHING

O CREATE !!!

O MAKE A GIFT PACK FOR YOUR FUTURE SELF

O START A BLOG

O SUPPORT YOUR LOCAL SPORTS|EVENTS|ARTISTS

O CRY IF YOU WANT TO

O FALL IN LOVE (WITH YOURSELF)

Chapter Ten

UNITED IN DIVERSITY

We are all unique; I don't have to tell you that. But what is it that makes us special really?

STEREOTYPE ALERT!

A *stereotype* is a widely held but fixed and oversimplified image of a particular person or group of people. Stereotypes are basically judgments we make about things or people without actually knowing them. Stereotypes usually revolve around race, gender, and culture. You've probably heard these stereotypes (or versions of them) before:

• Men should be leaders.

• Americans are lazy and obese.

• All muslims are terrorists.

• Blond girls are dumb.

• All models have anorexia.

• Gay men are feminine.

• Millennials mess everything up in our society.

Almost every culture has its own stereotypes. Stereotyping, however, can be hurtful. Even if a stereotype is positive, using it still means you're labeling people without knowing them. Try not to base your opinion of someone or a group of people on stereotypes alone: mingle and talk with different people from different backgrounds and places. That way, you can decide for yourself what that person is like based on your own experiences instead of merely making assumptions based on known stereotypes.

SUBCULTURES: THE FACTS

A subculture or a social group is, as the name already suggests, a sub-category of a larger culture. Subcultures are often all about exploring who you are and discovering what you stand for. As teenagers, we create our identities as we're growing up. Exploring our values is a very important part of adolescence and a way of finding the people who think and behave the same as we do.

THE SUBCULTURES THAT INFLUENCED ME

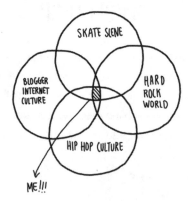

Different social groups each have their own unwritten guidelines on how to act, think, and dress. If you find a group that makes you feel comfortable, you may want to adapt the same behaviors and dress code to give you a strong bond and sense of belonging. Finding a group to be a part of can boost your social skills and, in general, it's super fun to feel accepted by people who are just like you.

I remember being a skater girl when I was a teenager. I dressed like the skaters, behaved like them, and talked like them. My family was convinced that it was just a phase, and it turned out they were right. But fortunately, my parents let me experiment and try things out to find my place. Being a part of the skater community taught me important things that I still remember and use today. The skaters were genuine and welcoming. They respected everyone, newbie or not. Overall, they were very open and social. Those are key characteristics I still carry in me, almost eight years later.

People young and old need to feel validated and valued. The following are a couple examples of just a few different subcultures you might find yourself a part of:

- **Gamer:** Gamers usually game together after school, whether online or offline, and they often talk about games during lunch or play games at school, too.
- **Goth:** A subculture that started in the 1980s and originally revolved around listening to goth music. Goth people typically adopt certain stylistic features, such as black clothing and black-dyed hair. They usually listen to gothic rock but are also open to other music genres such as post-punk, death rock, industrial, and so on.
- **Cyberculture:** Another name for computer culture, this is a subculture that is emerging from the use of computer networks (online communities, multiplayer gaming, social gaming, apps). Members of a cyberculture like to engage with political, sociological, and psychological issues that arise from networked interactions.
- **Emo:** A subculture that is characterized by an emphasis on emotional expression, an "emo" is someone who likes to dress in emo fashion (usually black clothes, T-shirts with emo band names, studded belts, sneakers), displays rather emotional characteristics, and usually listens to a type of rock music that's known for its expressive, emotional, and confessional lyrics. Emo people have their own defining style but are often confused with goths.

- **Hip-hop:** A subculture and art movement, originally developed by African Americans from the South Bronx during the late 1970s. Hip-hop is characterized by a number of elements, including rapping, break dancing, b-boying and b-girling, and spray-paint art (graffiti). Clothing and hair styles have always been a big part of hip-hop's image since its inception. Hip-hop clothing styles have changed over the decades but can generally be described as urban, baggy street wear.
- **Hipster:** This is someone who usually listens to indie and alternative music and likes to sin against all existing fashion rules, thereby creating their own fashion statements. A lot of hipster fashion items can be found in thrift stores. Hipsters generally have an alternative lifestyle; they are more likely to be progressive and enjoy organic or vegan food.

Of course, there are a bunch of other subcultures and social groups you might find yourself in: anime fandom, fitness or bodybuilding, cosplaying, furry fandom, glam rock, grunge rock, hacker culture, high culture, hippies, pinup and vintage clothing, role-playing gamers, ravers, skaters, riot grrrls, scouting, science-fiction fandom, surfers, straight edge, vampire lifestyle, and many more.

Identifying with a certain subculture might lead to some friction between you and your parents, especially if they aren't so supportive of the subculture you identify with. It could be the music you listen to, the way you dress, or how you talk or behave. Usually this happens because your parents don't know a lot about the friends you hang out with or about the values you all share. Try to involve your parents in the things that interest you, so they can get a general idea of what it is that interests you and so they won't be so sceptical about your choices and friend groups. Always be respectful, and don't expect your parents to understand your subculture in the blink of an eye. Give them time to adapt to your way of dressing and to your interests and ideas. It might be hard to imagine, but chances are your parents were part of a subculture as teens, too—and maybe they still are! Ask questions on how and what they did back in the day and see if you might find some common ground with them that you didn't know you had.

FIVE THINGS TO KEEP IN MIND WHEN ARGUING WITH SOMEONE YOU DON'T AGREE WITH

Unnecessary fights are never fun, especially if you're fighting over something that is hard to find common ground on. You can try as hard as you might to convince the other person you're right; the other person will try to do the exact same thing. In the previous chapter, you can read some of the best ways to express your opinion without being rude or hurting another person's feelings.

Imagine you're having an argument with someone, be it your spouse, friend, parent, or boss. Try to remember these five things when disagreeing with another person:

1. Don't let your anger get the best of you. Don't start calling the other person names. You'll soon regret it and won't find it productive to your argument. If you feel yourself losing control, count to ten in your head, take a deep breath, and think about what you want to say before blurting it out. If that doesn't help, ask for a quick break so you can compose yourself before continuing the argument.

2. Listen first, instead of thinking about a good comeback. You'll be able to give a better and more specific reply to their arguments if you take the time to listen to what they are actually saying.

3. Don't bring up past mistakes the other person may have made, especially if they're already water under the bridge. They have *nothing* to do with the argument you're having now and will only make you sound petty in your debate with them.

4. Don't randomly change the subject until you're done discussing the topic at hand. It's okay to decide to agree to disagree but don't end the argument until you feel that both sides have had their say.

5. People miscommunicate, and misunderstandings happen. Arguments can, in fact, be healthy sometimes. Being willing to admit culpability will teach you much more than you would think.

In general, just don't be a jerk when you are arguing with someone else. Don't punch the other person below the belt and always treat them the way you want to be treated: with R.E.S.P.E.C.T.

To learn more about arguing without anger, I suggest you read the following: *The Dance of Anger: A Woman's Guide to Changing the Patterns of Intimate Relationships* by Harriet Lerner and *Nonviolent Communication: A Language of Life: Life-Changing Tools for Healthy Relationships* by Marshall B. Rosenberg.

FIGHTING FOR EQUALITY EVEN IF IT FEELS USELESS

Often we might feel like we are in a constant balancing act—trying to do what's right and feeling dejected because our efforts don't seem to be making a difference. This can lead you to lose the motivation to keep fighting (and to possibly lose your faith in all humanity).

Let's face the facts: all of us aren't born equal. In a social context, this means that all of us aren't given the exact same chances. When we use the word *equality* in this context, we're talking about the equality of opportunity. No people, whatever their origin or skin color, should ever be denied participation in social institutions.

LITTLE JUSTICE WARRIOR

Other than a society of equal chances, what are some of the things you would like to see changed to make the world a more equal place? Imagine if what you want became a reality: how would you feel? Happy? Satisfied? At peace? What if I told you that the only thing needed to make that change is action from people who support it . . . people like you? Yes, you *are* able to make that change, if you want it enough.

It seems as if this life requires us to fight a lot for all sorts of things: for the people we love, for our health, for our jobs, and for bringing about social change. Where do we find the courage and the energy to keep fighting when it's so easy to just give up on something that is not easy to accomplish?

Stay focused on the solution and remind yourself what you're fighting for, which will help you stay productive. Also, don't be afraid to lose the first few battles before you see any improvement. Any change you inspire, no matter how small, is change and should be celebrated.

But how do we even now if something's worth fighting for? Ask yourself whether the situation you're in is so distressing that it needs to be addressed. If the answer is yes, you go ahead and fight. However, don't start any battle unless you do it in a constructive way.

THE ABCS OF THE LGBTQ

The abbreviation LGBTQ stands for lesbian, gay, bisexual, transgender, and queer or questioning. The acronym denotes a community of people across the entire spectrum of possible sexual orientations and gender identities. People often use the short version (LGBT or LGBTQ), when they actually mean to include all the different groups within LGBTTT-QQIA+. Let's take a look what each letter stands for:

Lesbian: A female homosexual, someone who has romantic or sexual feelings toward other women.

Gay: Primarily refers to a homosexual man (who has romantic or sexual feelings toward other men), but lesbians can also be referred to as gay.

Bisexual: Someone who is attracted, romantically and/or sexually, to both women and men—or to people with any other type of gender identity (sometimes termed pansexual).

Transgender: Umbrella term for people whose gender differs from the gender that is typically associated with the sex they were assigned at birth. In many cases, this is shortened to the word *trans*.

Transsexual: Someone with an inconsistent gender identity. They are usually not culturally associated with the sex they were assigned at birth.

Two-spirited: Umbrella term used to describe gender-variant individuals who don't conform to gender norms held by their communities (specifically people within indigenous communities).

Queer: Umbrella term for sexual and gender minorities.

Questioning: Someone who's exploring his or her gender, sexual identity, orientation, or all three at once.

Intersex: Variation in sex characteristics including chromosome, gonads, or genitals that do not allow for someone to be distinctly identified as male or female.

Asexual: Also known as nonsexual, this is someone who has little or no interest in sexual activity or has a lack of sexual attraction to anyone.

Additional terms in use also include:

Pansexual or Omnisexual: This is someone who has romantic, emotional, or sexual feelings for people of any sex or gender. They may refer to themselves as gender blind.

Agender or Genderless or Gender-Free: These people are those who self-identify as having no gender at all (basically they do not conform to traditional gender norms).

Gender Queer: Umbrella term for gender identities that are not strictly masculine or feminine but include configurations outside the gender binary.

Bigender: Gender identity where someone moves between feminine and masculine identities and behaviors.

Gender Variant or Gender Nonconformity: This describes behavior that doesn't match with masculine and feminine gender norms.

Pangender: Someone who identifies as all genders.

Ally: Anyone who considers him- or herself a friend of the LGBTQ+ community.

A person's gender identity indicates whether that person feels male, female, transgender, or none of the above, regardless of his or her biological sex (which is traditionally determined by having a penis or a vagina). *Gender expression* is a person's expression of his or her gender identity through the way he or she dresses or behaves.

The above list is constantly growing and evolving, so you don't have to memorize all the different definitions. As long as you use the preferred terms and pronouns, and do so respectfully, you'll be paying the LGBTQ+ community the respect it deserves.

ENRICHING YOUR LIFE THROUGH OTHER CULTURES

Learning about the habits, foods, practices, politics, and rituals of a culture can be an invaluable life lesson and experience. Knowing how different people live can deepen your understanding of the many cultures of this world. Whether it is through traveling, reading, being an exchange student, or having a best friend with a different cultural background, there are tons of ways to get a taste of a culture that is not yours.

Here's my list of arguments for why you should actively learn about new cultures and ways of doing things:

1. It teaches you to think in new ways. As a baby and a kid, you learn things the way they are taught to you (and typically as is considered normal for your culture). It's interesting to know how other people learn the same things in a different way. Understanding different approaches to life is always enriching.

2. You'll understand more about the world. When you see for yourself how other people eat, dress, and generally live their lives, you develop empathy for them. Many problems and wars are the result of ignorance and misunderstanding and a lack of empathy. If you give others a chance, they'll have respect for you in return.

3. You'll understand why cultural differences are important to all of us. The way we think and solve problems is not the only way. If we work together, we can combine ideas and technologies to solve problems.

4. It's just super interesting. Showing an interest in different cultures helps reduce racism and prejudice, too. You don't have to travel to learn more about the world, either. Even if you can't physically visit other cultures, you can still read books, watch documentaries, search the Internet, and learn from discussions with other people who have visited or who grew up in a different cultural setting.

5. It's fun and enjoyable. It's exercise for your mind, and it can be very entertaining. Learning a new language, eating different foods, exploring different habits . . . all of these expand your horizons and you may find something you really connect with, too.

Some people feel the need to openly express their intolerant attitudes and feelings toward other cultures. If someone has an irrational fear or hatred of foreigners, that's called *xenophobia*. Unfortunately, xenophobia can sometimes lead to violence and discrimination. Xenophobia is more common than we think, and it can affect pretty much everybody in the circle of people who surround you. Xenophobia often happens because people aren't aware of what goes on in the world outside their comfort zones. They are, quite simply, afraid of things they don't know.

A lot of those negative feelings are inspired by the images of different cultures that media spreads. If xenophobes would switch off their televisions or computers and actually get to know the people they're so afraid of, they'd most likely find that people are generally pretty similar across cultures. They might have slightly different takes on certain aspects of life, but the fact that we're all human beings means there's always common ground to be found. A major problem with xenophobia is that many people aren't open to learning about other cultures; they're much too stubborn to consider changing their opinions and moving beyond their prejudices.

Another major problem in combating cultural differences lies in miscommunication, which then can lead to irrational fears or even hatred. However, it's easy to avoid such misunderstandings by learning more about how people in other countries or cultures communicate, both verbally and nonverbally.

It's always important to remember that there are big differences between individual members of a culture, in the same way that all Americans are far from one stereotyped version. Maybe, just maybe, your world will have a little more color and feel a bit more peaceful if you open yourself up to exploring all the beautiful cultures in it.

I TRIED SEVERAL BREAKFASTS FROM AROUND THE GLOBE AND I LOVED THEM!

(TYPKAL)
SOME BREAKFASTS FROM DIFFERENT CULTURES AROUND THE GLOBE

POLAND : JAJECZNICA

ENGLAND: FULL ENGLISH BREAKFAST

SPAIN :(QUICK) PAN CON TOMATE

MOROCCO: BAGHIR AND OTHER DELICIOUS BREADS

ICELAND : HAFRAGRAUTUR

  AUSTRALIA: TOAST AND VEGEMITE

 PORTUGAL: CROISSANTS AND COFFEE

(US) AMERICA: PANCAKES AND BACON

INDIA: ROSEMARY POTATOES, INDIAN TOFU SCRAMBLE

 RUSSIA : OLADI

BOLIVIA: SALTENAS

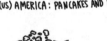

THAILAND :KHAW PAD KAI

EGYPT : FOUL MADAMAS

JAPAN : TOFU IN SOYA

 KOREA: SOUP AND KIMCHI

PAKISTAN: ALOO PARATHA

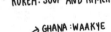 GHANA :WAAKYE

 COSTA RICA: GALLO PINTO

VENEZUELA: EMPANADAS

 CHINA : NOODLES

HOW CAN I EMBRACE MY DIFFERENCE AS A STRENGTH?

We are all different. We have different abilities and talents. We have different tastes in music and fashion. We don't always agree on politics or on which TV shows we like. We have different skin tones, hair types, and eye color. Some of us like boys; some of us like girls; some of us like both; and others prefer something in between. Some of us are differently abled. Others struggle to find their own identities. You get my point—we're all unique and special in some way, right? But then, what makes it so easy for us to admire other people's abilities and accept their quirks but so hard to embrace our own?

Let's agree that no one has any business deciding what we should look like, ever. Still, we convince ourselves that endless compliments and jealous looks from others is what we need in order to love who we are. We constantly compare ourselves to others, and it's making us sad, angry, and, most of all, tired. Because we can't, and never will be, like the person we want to be. We can only be ourselves.

We are so forgiving and accepting toward others, but so unforgiving for ourselves. Since I became unapologetic about myself, started putting myself first at times, and learned how to take care of myself, I've discovered that those are the most important things we should be doing. Sometimes I wonder if other people experience the same feelings. I wonder if my cousin in Thailand worries about the same things at night. Sometimes I even feel guilty because I think I'm worrying about stuff that doesn't *really* matter. I mean, I have a home, a beautiful job, a wonderful group of friends, and a great guy by my side. What more could I possibly want from this super awesome, privileged life?

Repeat after me: "It's not a crime to like myself." In fact, it's perfectly cool to like yourself and the way you look. How often do you say the words, "I love and approve of myself" out loud? Never?

Chapter Ten: United in Diversity

Try it. I know it sounds super corny the first time, but that's because the idea of accepting yourself makes you uncomfortable. Never underestimate the power of giving yourself a good pep talk from time to time.

Do the things that you like. How often do you refrain from doing something you really want to do just because you're afraid that other people might think it's silly or that you'll look stupid? It took me many years to work up the courage to buy the clothes I liked, to wear the makeup I thought looked cute, or to openly wear a bikini. I turned things around for myself because I woke up one day thinking, *what if I just did the things that I've been dreaming about?* Things like wearing cute clothes, experimenting with makeup and accessories, and, most important, embracing my heritage. What did I have to lose? Absolutely nothing. As it turned out, none of it was as scary as I'd feared, and the only person who'd been holding me back all that time was . . . me. I know my body and looks are different from my friends', but that's exactly what makes me *me*.

These are a couple of people who inspire me on a daily basis and who remind me that we should all be a little nicer to ourselves, regardless of how we look:

- **@bodypositivememes:** The girl behind this meme page is very inspirational and makes YouTube videos, as well. Even if the body-positive movement in general seems mostly focused on girls who are curvy or plus-sized, this girl tries to make sure she includes all types of women in her content.
- **@slaythepatriarchy:** Reminding members of the LGBTQ+ community (and everyone else, too) to love and embrace themselves, no matter how they self-identify.
- **@kinglimaa:** A model with a hijab, proving that beauty comes in all shapes and religions.
- **@mdmflow:** Cruelty-free makeup for people with different skin tones, created in response to the lack of diversity in the makeup industry.
- **@womencanplay:** A nonprofit organization powered by volunteers

that promotes sports and creates opportunities for women and girls to get active.

- **@upandoutcomic**: Awesomely beautiful, moving, and relatable comics about a transgender woman sharing her everyday experiences.
- **@bretmanrock**: An Internet icon who proves that makeup knows no gender by creating hilariously entertaining videos in which he shows his stunning talent.
- **@lavernecox**: You may know her from the Netflix series *Orange Is the New Black*, but she's so much more than a seriously talented actress—she's also an active advocate for transgender rights.
- **@yesimhotinthis**: Hilarious webcomic about the misadventures of a slightly sweaty Muslim American woman.

All of the people on this list use their platform to inspire others, and it's truly wonderful to see how many people they've helped on their way toward self-acceptance. Whether it's through modeling, photos, blog posts, comedy, videos, art, or comics, these creators have embraced themselves and have made it their mission to help others accomplish the same. If you're struggling to accept your looks and are trying to learn how to turn your unique qualities into real strenghts, having a role model can help you a lot. Even I created a YouTube video on how I stopped having negative thoughts about myself. It is called "You Are Awesome—11 Tips and Tricks to Realize That," and you can find it on my YouTube channel (Chrostin).

I have talked enough about myself now. It's your time to shine and to change all the negative, toxic self-talk in your head and learn the most empowering magic trick in the world: to love and appreciate yourself. If we all start doing this, then maybe the world will be slightly more united in its diversity. But as you know, every big change starts small. So do that small thing: accept yourself.

The time is now. Start today.

RESOURCES
AND REFERENCES

AAUW: American Association of University Women. "Fight for Fair Pay." Retrieved from http://www.aauw.org/fairpay/.

AAUW: American Association of University Women. "The Simple Truth about the Gender Pay Gap." (Spring 2017). Retrieved from http://www.aauw.org/research/the-simple-truth-about-the-gender-pay-gap/.

Barber, N. "Do Humans Need Meat?" (October 12, 2016). [Blog post]. Retrieved from https://www.psychologytoday.com/blog/the-human-beast/201610/do-humans-need-meat.

Barnsen, J. "4 Signs You May Be Facing Employment Discrimination." (January 27, 2014). Retrieved from https://www.workitdaily.com/employment-discrimination-signs/.

Blanchard, A. M. *The American Urge to Censor: Freedom of Expression Versus the Desire to Sanitize Society —— From Anthony Comstock to 2 Live Crew* (1992). Retrieved from http://scholarship.law.wm.edu/cgi/viewcontent.cgi?article=1897&context=wmlr.

Boogaard, K. "6 Smart Ways to Disagree with Someone Respectfully." [Blog post]. (September 29, 2016). Retrieved from https://www.inc.com/kat-boogaard/6-key-tips-to-respectfully-disagree-with-someone.html.

Bratskeir, K. "Man Describes Immense Torture of Eating Only Ramen for 30 Days." (September 25, 2014). Retrieved from http://www.huffingtonpost.com/2014/09/25/ramen-diet-man-eats-so-many-noodles_n_5874776.html.

Cavanagh, C. "Why We Still Need Feminism." [Blog post]. (September 18, 2014). Retrieved from http://www.huffingtonpost.com/casey-cavanagh/why-we-still-need-feminism_b_5837366.html.

CDC: Center for Disease Control and Prevention. "Lesbian, Gay, Bisexual, and Transgender Health." Retrieved from https://www.cdc.gov/lgbthealth/youth.htm.

Chung, M. "Have You Ever Felt Like You Don't Fit In?" [Blog post]. Retrieved from https://introvertspring.com/ever-felt-like-dont-fit/.

CMCH: Mental Health Center. "Fighting Fair to Resolve Conflict." Retrieved from https://cmhc.utexas.edu/fightingfair.html#5.

Engels, J. "10 Ways to Experience a Culture Authentically while Traveling." [Blog post]. (August 28, 2013). Retrieved from http://www.transitionsabroad.com/listings/travel/articles/10-ways-travel-abroad-experience-culture.shtml.

EOC. "What Is Discrimination?" Retrieved from http://www.eoc.org.uk/what-is-discrimination/.

Fawcett Society. "We Are a Nation of Hidden Feminists." (January 15, 2016). Retrieved from https://www.fawcettsociety.org.uk/news/we-are-a-nation-of-hidden-feminists.

Gallo, A. "Choose the Right Words in an Argument." (June 16, 2014). Retrieved from https://hbr.org/2014/06/choose-the-right-words-in-an-argument.

Jackson, K. "Understanding Other Cultures Has Broad Benefits." [Blog post]. (August 27, 2008). Retrieved from http://munews.missouri.edu/news-releases/2008/0827-heppner-apa%20award.php.

LGBT Helpline. "What Is LGBT?" Retrieved from http://lgbt.ie/about/what-is-lgbt?.

LifeBuzz. "13 Famous Celebrities Tell The Truth about the Fame And Happiness." (March, 2016). Retrieved from http://www.lifebuzz.com.

Lips, K. A. "Don't Buy into the Gender Pay Gap." [Blog post]. (April 12, 2016). Retrieved from https://www.forbes.com/sites/karinagness/2016/04/12/dont-buy-into-the-gender-pay-gap-myth/#460a0a125969.

Madden, M., Lenhart, A., Cortesi, S., Gasser, U., Duggan, M., Smith, A., & Beaton, M. "Teens, Social Media and Privacy." (2013). Retrieved from http://www.pewinternet.org/2013/05/21/teens-social-media-and-privacy/.

Markman, A. "Ask The Experts: I Think I'm Being Discriminated Against for Having A Baby." (April 2, 2015). Retrieved from https://www.fastcompany.com/3041864/ask-the-experts-is-my-company-is-discriminating-against-me-for-having-a-baby.

Marquit, M. "5 Reasons to Learn about Different Cultures." [Blog post]. Retrieved from https://liverichlivewell.com/learn-about-different-cultures/.

Matthews, S. "5 Reasons Why You Should Be a Feminist." [Blog post]. (March 11, 2017). Retrieved from https://www.hercampus.com/school/falmouth/5-reasons-why-you-should-be-feminist.

Miller, T. "My Strange Ramen Addiction: Teen Eats Almost Nothing but Noodles for 13 Years." (April 10, 2013) Retrieved from http://www.nydailynews.com/life-style/health/teen-eats-ramen-noodles-13-years-article-1.1312782.

Moore, M. "5 Reasons Your Teen Needs Breakfast." (January 21, 2014). [Blog post]. Retrieved from http://www.eatright.org/resource/food/nutrition/healthy-eating/5-reasons-your-teen-needs-breakfast.

Moss, M. Salt, Sugar, Fat: How the Food Giants Hooked US. (2014). New York: Random House.

National Women's Law Center. The Wage Gap. Retrieved from https://www.infoplease.com/us/gender-sexuality/wage-gap.

Nemko, M. "When You Don't Fit In." [Blog post]. (September 24, 2014). Retrieved from https://www.psychologytoday.com/blog/how-do-life/201409/when-you-don-t-fit-in.

Ok2beme. What Does LGBTQ+ Mean? (July 24, 2017). Retrieved from http://ok2bme.ca/resources/kids-teens/what-does-lgbtq-mean/.

PETA. Simply. Live. Consciously. [Video file]. (2016). Retrieved from https://www.youtube.com/watch?time_continue=54&v=Ie3FyDsYFlw.

Petridis, A. "Youth Subcultures: What Are They Now?" (March 20, 2014). Retrieved from https://www.theguardian.com/culture/2014/mar/20/youth-subcultures-where-have-they-gone.

Pursue Action.org. "The Benefits of Learning about Other Cultures." [Blog post]. (May 20, 2016). Retrieved from http://www.pursueaction.org/benefits-learning-cultures/.

Raising Children.net. Teenagers and Youth Subcultures. Retrieved from http://raisingchildren.net.au/articles/subcultures.html.

Raja, D. "Top 25 Easy and Healthy Breakfasts for Teens." [Blog post]. (January 6, 2017). Retrieved from http://www.momjunction.com/articles/healthy-breakfast-ideas-for-your-teen_00348110/#gre.

Resources and References

Scott, E. "International Women's Day: Why More and More Young People Are Calling Themselves Feminists." (March 8, 2017). Retrieved from http://metro.co.uk/2017/03/08/international-womens-day-why-more-and-more-young-people-are-calling-themselves-feminists-6495228/.

Sezen, T. "What's the Difference between Romantic and Sexual Orientation?" (2016). Retrieved from https://vocaladymagazine.com.

Steber, C. "11 Reasons You Feel Like You Don't Fit It & What To Do About It." [Blog post]. (August 10, 2016). Retrieved from https://www.bustle.com/articles/173740-11-reasons-you-feel-like-you-dont-fit-in-what-to-do-about-it.

Steen, J. "This Is Why Junk Food Tastes So Bloody Good." (December 21, 2016). Retrieved from http://www.huffingtonpost.com.au/2016/12/20/this-is-why-junk-food-tastes-so-bloody-good_a_21632106/.

Symantec Corporation (US). "Why Your Online Privacy Matters." Retrieved from https://us.norton.com/internetsecurity-privacy-why-your-online-privacy-matters.html.

TEDx. *We Should All Be Feminists*. [Video file]. (2013). Retrieved from https://www.ted.com/talks/chimamanda_ngozi_adichie_we_should_all_be_feminists/details.

Teen Talk. "Discrimination." Retrieved from http://teentalk.ca/hot-topics/appreciating-diversity-2/discrimination/.

Thierer, A. "Why Do We Always Sell the Next Generation Short?" [Blog post]. (January 8, 2012). Retrieved from https://www.forbes.com/sites/adamthierer/2012/01/08/why-do-we-always-sell-the-next-generation-short/#4ae1a8342d75.

Tudge, C. *Neanderthals, Bandits and Farmers: How Agriculture Really Began*. (1999). New Haven, CT, US: Yale University Press.

VOMNCK. "The Negative Connotation of the Word 'Feminism' Explained." [Blog post]. (March 4, 2013). Retrieved from https://vomnck.wordpress.com/2013/03/04/the-negative-connotation-of-the-word-feminism-explained/.

Vox. *What People Miss about the Gender Wage Gap*. [Video file]. (September 7, 2016). Retrieved from https://www.youtube.com/watch?v=13XU4fMIN3w.

WaterCure. "Frequently Asked Questions." (2008). Retrieved from http://www.watercure.com/faq.html.

Weiss, S. "6 Reasons People Believe Stereotypes about Feminists Even Though They're not True." [Blog post]. (December 29, 2015). Retrieved from https://www.bustle.com/articles/132468-6-reasons-people-believe-stereotypes-about-feminists-even-though-theyre-not-true.

Witherly, S. A. "Why Humans Like Junk Food." (2013). Retrieved from http://jamesclear.com/wp-content/uploads/2013/11/why-humans-like-junk-food-steven-witherly.pdf?x25662.

Wikipedia.org. "List of Subcultures." Retrieved from https://en.wikipedia.org/wiki/List_of_subcultures.

Workplace Gender Equality Agency. "What Is the Gender Pay Gap?" Retrieved from https://www.wgea.gov.au/addressing-pay-equity/what-gender-pay-gap.

Zaraska, M. *Meathooked: The History and Science of Our 2.5-Million Year Obsession with Meat*. (2016). New York: Basic Books.

A (CHEESY) SPECIAL THANKS

I would love to take this moment to thank a couple of awesome human beings who helped me with realizing this book.

Firstly, thank you to Mark Gottlieb for giving me this amazing opportunity and supporting me along the way. A special thanks to my all-female team at Running Press, especially Julie and Frances, for their sincere guidance and help for completing this work. You've taken a chance on me, and I hope I made it totally worth it. To Elise Joris, for running the final sprint with me. We had a few intense weeks, but I'm happy I shared them with you.

A special mention to Miss Liliane Priem, probably the best teacher a student can wish for, always telling me not to give up. Thank you for keeping me on the right track at school and giving me a million chances when I mess up.

My family and friends: for always supporting my ambitions, both financially and mentally. Peter, who is my accountant, my assistant, advisor, and dad. To my best friends: you guys rock. When I'm rich, I'll pay you back all the drinks you've advanced.

To my girl Emmelien, to whom I have dedicated this book. Em, you stood by me since day one. Without you, I would not be writing this page at the moment.

My sweetheart, Mikel, for all your kindness, support, and providing the right snacks.

To all the girls and women around the globe who (indirectly) inspired me to write this book: you are the future.

And finally, to all the people who are offended because they didn't make this page: you mean a lot to me! You are supporting a young woman's dream and that's the best thing *ever*.